Gita Saar

A New Perspective

Arun Kumar Kapur

INDIA • SINGAPORE • MALAYSIA

ISBN
Paperback 979-8-89133-401-4
Hardcase 979-8-89133-425-0

Dedicated to my respected late father, Sh Hans Raj Kapur and my respected late mother, Smt Vimla Rani Kapur. Without their blessings this work was not possible.

AUTHOR'S NOTE

In the year 2000, my late father, Sh Hans Raj Kapur, gifted me a copy of Shrimadbhagwad Gita – Sadhak Sanjivani by Swami Ramsukhdas. The book, with elaborate explanations of each shloka and its explanatory writeups, became the starting point and inspiration for my Gita journey. That book also became the foundation and the building block for the book in your hands. A non-conventional approach has been chosen in this book to present the message of Gita wherein, instead of explanation for each shloka, subject matter has been presented topic-wise with relevant gist from all the chapters. I am honoured to draw inputs from 'Gita As It Is' by Swami Prabhupada, 'The Bhagwad Gita According to Gandhi' by Orient Publishing, New Delhi, 'Gyaneshwari' by Sant Gyaneshwar, 'Sadhak-Sudha-Sindhu' published by Gita Press, Gorakhpur and very inspiring writeups appearing in 'The Speaking Tree', a Times of India collection.

Gita shows us how every human being can come to adapt the subtle Vedanta principles in the day-to-day life. The Bhagwad Gita, as an invaluable guide, helps us to drive past our own barriers, refine our values and achieve excellence. It enables us to realise our true potential and makes us self-sufficient. Lord Krishna helped Arjun win a battle that he was least willing to undertake. Out of delusion, he had actually laid down his arms. The message of Gita is not restricted to the battlefield of Kurukshetra alone. Armed with the knowledge of Gita, we all can realise

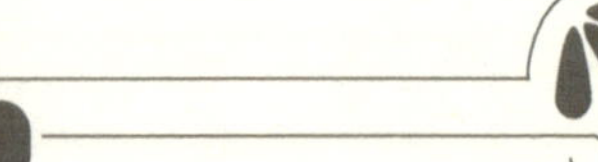

our potential and come out winner in every situation in life.

The young are usually looking for enjoyment and good times. Success, happiness and fulfilling relationships are on their wish list. Yet, depression, stress and anxiety are increasingly striking the young. They believe that the more possessions one has, more he will enjoy. So, they start chasing material things to create a false sense of enjoyment and happiness. Soon they realise that more they indulge, lesser they enjoy. Gita enables us to be happy as we are, where we are, without having to change anything around us. We only need to change our attitude. When the attitude shifts from grabbing to giving, from taking to contributing, we become creative, motivated and successful. Gita enables us to enjoy the world as well as rise above it. It prescribes regulated contact with sense objects. Success will come naturally, as an unintended side-effect.

No single book can cover the message of Gita, in its entirety. But I hope that this humble attempt is useful.

- Arun Kumar Kapur

CONTENTS

1

THE BODY AND THE SOUL

II As a person discarding worn out clothes puts on new ones, so an embodied soul, casting off old body, enters into another, which is new…Gita 2:22 II

There are millions of life forms on earth. Based on the laws of karma the souls keep transiting from one form of bodies to another, one life form to another, upgrading or downgrading. Considering that human form is the finest species right at the top of the ladder, do we say that karma of lower species is enabling them to earn human form? Scriptures may have answer to this. Each species has a role to play in the survival of other species. All living beings are born of the five great elements and finally merge into them for re-creation. This interplay of atoms is very complex process possibly beyond the comprehension of us mortals. Embodied Self in everyone is set on a great journey in which it comes to temporarily identify itself with different forms to gain a set of experiences. It is difficult to tell as to when and why this journey of the soul started, in the first place. To return to the Almighty the soul needs to go through various experiences to exhaust the fruits of past actions and for this it takes the help of a physical body. Selection of the body is decided based on accumulated karma and its need to gain new experiences on its spiritual journey.

The physical or perishable body is merely a vehicle used by the imperishable soul for

its spiritual journey towards realisation. Soul is essential for the body to have a living state and the body is essential for the embodied soul to go through the circumstances created as the fruits of action, and become free in its journey towards emancipation. To understand this, we need to first understand, what 'body' is and how the soul, or Self, is different from the body. A body functions on three planes –gross (*sthool*), subtle (*sookshm*) and causal (*kaaran*). Of these, only the gross body is visible to our eyes. The subtle and causal bodies can only be perceived.

The body which is nourished by food and water for its growth and sustenance is gross or physical body. The functions of the gross body involve actions and sensorial reactions. These actions and reactions occur at physical plane. The gross body consists of five elements –fire, water, air, earth, and ether. Gross body is not the Self as it is knowable by senses and it changes every moment, while the soul is free from all afflictions. Soul has no constituent elements. It is shapeless and changeless. The subtle body, on the other hand, includes senses, mind, and intellect. The subtle body can be perceived by intellect. The functions of the subtle body involve desires, emotions, ideas, and concrete thoughts. It functions at astral plane and is not a subject of intelligence. Subtle body is also not the Self as it changes every moment and is an object of knowledge. Causal body generally refers to the highest or the innermost body that veils the Soul. The function of the causal body involves ideals and abstract thoughts. It is at mental plane. The Self is beyond all these.

These bodies gain dominance at different stages of awareness, i.e., wakefulness, sleep and deep sleep. During wakefulness man has the capability to use full range and spectrum of all three bodies although within individual limitations. In sleep, there is predominance of subtle body. In sound sleep there is predominance of causal body. In this stage of deep sleep, person is neither aware of the gross body nor of subtle body. During sleep and deep sleep, the internal functions of the gross body, however, continue as usual.

As seeds sown in a field yield the corresponding crop in due course, seeds of actions which a man performs yield their fruit at an appointed time. The body is, thus, a field or '*Kshetra*'. It also includes emotions, thoughts, desires etc. Changes in physical body are visible and are easy to observe. The subtle body also changes, e.g., in sleep, a child sees himself as a child, youth as a youth and old man sees himself as an old man. There is a change in causal body also because in childhood one gets more sound sleep than in youth, and in old age it further decreases. Even though there are changes in the body as man passes through childhood, youth and old age, he experiences that he is the same person. It implies that there is no change in Self. When we rise after a sound sleep, we say that we slept soundly and that

we were not aware of anything during the sleep. This knowledge that we were not aware of anything, is of the Self or soul because soul exists continuously. Changes in sense organs are perceived by the mind. Changes in mind are perceived by the intellect. The changes in intellect, i.e. different levels of understanding, are known by the soul which always remains unchanged. soul is the real onlooker, knower, perceiver or *kshetragya* which can perceive and know others independently but can never be known or seen by anyone.

Soul is all pervading and stable. It has no shape because anything which has a shape will have limitation of its external boundary and, therefore, cannot pervade everywhere. It is thus homogeneous in its presence. Something which is all pervading and homogeneous must be stable and firm. It cannot shake or move, since movement implies transfer of an object from one set of time and place to another set of time and place, where it was not present earlier. Being all-pervasive, there is no place or space where soul is not present. Soul and body are like sea and its waves. Waves are born in the sea, they grow, weaken, and finally die away in the sea and the sea remains as it is.

It is not possible to describe the soul. It is unmanifest all the time. A thing is said to be manifest when we can perceive it through a sense organ. That which is beyond the perception of all the five sense organs, is called unmanifest. The unmanifest soul enables sense organs to perceive.

The soul is also incomprehensible by the mind and intellect. We cannot, therefore, give it a definition because it cannot be comprehended. Comprehension is the combined function of the brain in the gross body and of the mind and intellect in the subtle body. The soul being the very life, energises the mind and the intellect. It is, therefore, obvious that the mind and intellect cannot make the Self an object of their comprehension.

Soul is neutral. We know that Sun illuminates everything that appears in its light. It can be a holy act or a crime being committed. But it cannot be held responsible for any of those acts. Similarly, soul being eternal and neutral does not concern itself whether the life it illuminates, is involved in good activity or bad. It remains indifferent and unattached to these acts. The Truth exists forever but it is not comprehended due to darkness of ignorance. Inability to comprehend the Truth does not imply that Truth is non-existent. Like the object kept in darkness can be seen as soon as light is switched on, the realisation takes place as soon as the veil of ignorance on the Truth is removed.

The soul does not act. It is the nature which performs all actions and body is part of nature. Soul being subtler than the nature, the nature cannot cause soul to act.

It is the soul which enables nature to act and function. As electric current operates our radio, we appreciate the radio and the sound from it, completely forgetting to attach any importance to the electric current that has enabled the radio to function. Without electric current the radio would be merely a lifeless box. As soon as electricity is available, it begins to perform the assigned task. Same is the case with soul and the body.

Another example can be of the train that receives power from the engine. Without the steam or electricity to run it, the engine is useless. Engine has no senses, mind and intellect of its own. It therefore needs a driver with senses, mind and intellect. Man, on the other hand has an engine in the form of body and has senses, mind and intellect to drive it. So, it does not need a driver. But a light source is still necessary. Soul is this source. First the light is reflected in the intellect, from the intellect it goes to the mind, from mind it goes to the senses and then the body

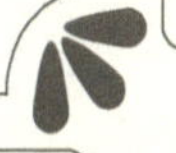

functions. Intellect, mind, senses and the body – these are modes and their illuminator is the soul which is not connected with them. The modes act on the modes while the soul is aloof and unattached.

Swami Prabhupada in his book 'Bhagavad-Gita As It Is', writes, "Each of us individually suffers because of crimes committed in another form, in a different locality, at a different period of time in the past, certainly there must be some identity between the sinner of the past and the sufferer in the present. This identity is the mind-intellect equipment in each one of us. At the time of death, the subtle body moves off gathering unto itself all faculties not in any gross form but as a mere fragrance of what all they had lived through, felt in and thought of. At the time of departing from the body, the subtle body gathers itself from the gross dwelling place, and on reaching the new physical structure, it spreads itself out again to use its faculties through that new house-of-experience".

The mind-intellect equipment records whatever a person does in his lifetime and this equipment stays with the soul till its emancipation. This equipment carries impressions and stores new experiences. When mind-intellect equipment finds that its embodiment in a given form cannot facilitate its evolution anymore, it considers the existing physical form as worn out. The age and health of the physical body does not matter. The current form is discarded and another physical form is taken up which would be most suited for it to gain the next required type of experiences. Problem is that a man is happy while discarding old clothes and putting on new ones, but he feels aggrieved when the soul decides to cast off an old body to get into a new one. This happens due to attachment because man wants to live forever thinking that the death of the body is the end of him.

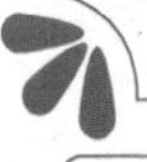

The soul is akin to the screen on which the movie is played. After all the violence, bloodshed, storms, emotions, tears in the movie the screen remains clean and intact once the movie is over. Similarly, the changeless and infinite soul becomes the platform on which the life's drama is played out. The motive is, however, recorded by the mind-intellect equipment and becomes the basis for determining the fruit of action. Soul is not blamed or appreciated for any action. The steam in the engine is not punished for the disaster of derailment, nor is the steam complimented when the train reaches its destination in time! Again, neither the disaster nor the successful accomplishment of the journey could ever take place without the steam.

It is commonly known as to what happens to our physical body when we die but what happens to our soul? Physical death means the release of our immortal soul from the confines of our mortal body. Depending upon the karma as recorded in the mind-intellect equipment and taking cognisance of the unexhausted fruits, it is assigned another body. To understand this merger, let us take the example of a room. The space in the room is a part of the unlimited space around the room. If the walls of the room crumble down, the space in the room merges with the space outside and the entire space returns to continuity. Once the soul is released from the body the *jivatma* and the space rejoin seamlessly. After death of the physical body the soul merges with the energy from which it was never separated.

One more example will further explain the relationship between the body, soul and Supersoul or God. Soul is an integral and indivisible part of the Supersoul or God. While soul exists inside a living body, the Supersoul that is all-pervading occupies the space outside. Both are formless and invisible. Soul has no birth or death; it is self-existent like God and does not intervene

in any movement or action of the body that it dwells in. Suppose we are standing in an open ground and sunlight is there all around. Now, when we enter a small room and keep the door open, sunlight from outside exists in the room also and we can see things as clearly as outside. This is the relation between soul and Supersoul. While the Supersoul is the sunlight prevailing outside, the soul is its integral part illuminating the room – that is, the body it dwells in from inside. Suppose we close the door from inside. There is darkness. The situation will get restored as soon as the door is opened or the very structure falls. Even though an undivided part of the Supersoul; the soul is incorrectly visualized as separated from it simply because the door is closed. With the darkness, the soul starts identifying itself with the body that it resides in. Darkness in the room does not mean that there is no light outside. It is the mind that closes the door and the soul gets engulfed by darkness. Connection with the outside light is restored as soon as the door is opened and the attachment with the room is removed. Finding the light is neither an invention nor a discovery. It is merely realization of what always exists.

Soul merging with the Supersoul or God is like two drops of water merging to form a larger drop. That larger entity retains the qualities, characteristics and property of the smaller drops but now exists as one entity. This newly formed larger drop, on falling into ocean would not exist in its original form, but all its molecules, atoms, properties and characteristics would still exist. It would have access to all the resources of the ocean. When we become one with God, we do not cease to exist. On the contrary, our consciousness expands. We will still retain every memory, thought, feeling that we have accumulated over several incarnations.

2

MODES OF NATURE

II Sattva, Rajas and Tamas – these gunas born of nature, bind the imperishable spirit to the body… Gita 14:5 II

Mode of nature or *Guna* means personality, innate nature and psychological attributes of an individual. There are three gunas that have always been present in all things and beings in the world. These three gunas are called: *sattva, rajas and tamas.* The interplay of these gunas defines the individual nature, individual values and also how that person would react and behave in a given situation and in dealings with others. It would also reflect on his decision making. Sattva is the quality of goodness, balance, purity, peace, compassion, and virtue. Rajas is the quality of passion, activity, confusion, and egoism. Tamas is the quality of darkness, chaos, delusion, inertia, negativity, and ignorance. These gunas co-exist but different gunas dominate at different times. One's nature and behaviour reflect on interplay of all three gunas. Gunas are dynamic and changeable but change in one guna forces inertia from other two gunas.

We have little control over our own capabilities and capacities that are dependent on gunas which, in turn, are shaped by impressions. These impressions are carried forward from the past life and are also accumulated in the present life. Impressions, or sanskars, are not gathered from parents alone. We continue to collect impressions

throughout our lifetime from individuals we meet, from school, from our work or business environment, from friends as well as opponents: in fact, from all circumstances we witness or go through. The five senses help us in picking up these impressions which, over a period, mature into *guna.* Karma determines the circumstances in our life which appear as fruit of our past actions while guna determines our personality and nature. All the dynamics and variety in the world is because of guna.

A person with dominant sattva guna cares for those who are frightened, intimidated by the ups and downs of life. Due to inherent gentleness in behaviour and affection for others, especially the weaker section, the tendency in sattva is to be very understanding and caring. Sattva guna is not rigid and involves willingness to lose ground, if necessary, for the sake of others. Person with dominant sattva guna is constantly involved in action and never considers fruit of action as motivation or discouragement. Rajas people, on the other hand, stop trusting anyone but themselves and consider others either as a tool to achieve what they want or as a threat to fulfilment of their desires. In rajas, the tendency is to dominate, impress and show off. Aggression towards others becomes an essential tool. Energy, in rajas, is always directed towards achieving personal glory and praise. Tamas guna stops us from thinking and applying our mind to the situation. In tamas the tendency is to remain lazy and delude. In the famous 'half glass full-half glass empty' situation sattva sees the full portion and is contented, rajas sees the empty part and does everything in the power to fill it and show others that he has done it. Tamas, in its delusion and laziness possibly does not even see the glass.

Each guna has its primary identifiable characteristics. Sattva implies scholarship, rajas stands for leadership and entrepreneurship and tamas is identified with laziness and servitude. But due to interplay these are not rigid classifications. There are scholars who are rajasik or tamasik; there are servants who are rajasik or even sattvik. There are leaders who with their sattvik qualities stand out and leaders with tamasik qualities become corrupt. Such people are found in every community and walk of life. Guna will continuously make people take decisions that even their mind does not support. Gunas remain dormant but manifest in the words, actions, thoughts, inter-personal relations and demonstrated behaviour, whenever a person gets involved in worldly affairs.

While judging a person we should be considerate towards his gunas. Opinion should not be formed too quickly. If we can appreciate the dominant guna, we will be more open and considerate while judging. That way we connect with the soul and our judgement is more rational. If we do not do this, we become victim of ego which will cloud our judgement. We should remember

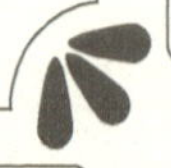

that while judging, our own gunas also come into play. With ego, we fail to appreciate the power of guna and blame others for our problems.

The elements of the nature are standard everywhere. Medical science would have been helpless if the human body was not standardised. Everyone has the same senses and sense organs and these function in an identical manner. The vitalising spirit is same in everyone. We breathe in the same oxygen and breathe out the same carbon di-oxide. The minerals and the gases do not change their properties with region. Despite similar resources being available to everyone, it is a surprise that we find so many varieties among humans, animals, plants and other living beings. This variety comes from the gunas which decide how an individual's mind functions. Only a person who can appreciate the gunas and their influence, can manage them to achieve self-control.

Naturally, everyone would like to acquire sattvik guna and lead a very pious and peaceful life, Due to tribulations of life it is not easy for a person to achieve this, even though it is not impossible. With conscious effort, it is possible to achieve dominant sattvik guna by a person with dominant tamasik guna. He must first realise the dominant guna in him. A tamasik person will first have to shake off the lethargy and overcome the delusion. Rajasik person can also achieve the same by overcoming desire, ego, and attachment. Person must allow the dormant divine tendencies in him to manifest themselves.

Due to its attachment to body, the soul considers itself performing all the actions and thus, becomes part of individual's life journey. The soul is supposed to be a silent observer but due to attachment, it becomes the doer. Due to this assumed doership, it does not achieve liberation and must keep returning to the material world to receive the fruits of past actions. That is why, while it is said that one who is born will certainly die, it is said with equal certainty that one who dies will be born again. The gunas, born of impressions, lead to attachment and thus the actions become karma. While performing action, interacting with the material world and while going through the circumstances appearing as fruit of past actions, one gathers more impressions. These impressions form gunas leading to further karma. The cycle continues and it needs consistent effort to come out of it. One must realise that it is gunas which are acting on gunas and he should not get affected with this interplay.

For emancipation, one needs to rise above the three modes of nature. It may not be easy to transcend all gunas but we must remain unaffected in desirable and undesirable circumstances, which appear in our lives as fruits of past actions. Honour and dishonour should be equal for us and we should neither be pleased in praise nor displeased in blame. We should be constantly established in

Self. We should be able to identify value or importance of everything around us but should remain unaffected in their gain or their loss. Mahatma Gandhi has said, "He who transcends the three gunas, does not suffer when any of them predominates over the others – and does not desire that one of these should prevail or subside. The state beyond the three gunas can only be imagined. It does not seem possible to maintain it in action. In concrete action, our state must be sattvik to the highest degree."

Gunas bind soul to the body in different ways as all three gunas have binding characteristics of their own. As against the common belief, Sattva can also be binding. The happiness realised due to sattva can lead to pride and bind the soul. Rajas is identified with desire and action and both are binding. Rajogun enhances desire and attachment while desire and attachment enhance rajogun. Unless the link is broken, the relationship continues perpetually. Tamas is binding by itself, because of ignorance, delusion, and lack of discrimination,

Rajas is the most prevalent guna in this material world. All non-spiritual activities including social, economic, political, and religious, fall in the domain of rajas. The common man's struggle in life is propelled by rajasik tendencies like selfishness, aggression, and greed. Rajasik people appear to be efficient but their real motivation lies in ensuring benefit for themselves and their near and dear ones. They celebrate their acquisitions of wealth and power to show off. They may not possess plenty but always feel the need to pretend. They are always worried and stressed about possible loss. Hypocrisy, attachment, desire-prompted devotion, all these also fall in the domain of rajasik. Rajasik people observe rituals that prevail in society, not for their spiritual advancement but for protecting their acquisitions and asking for more. Rajasik people give donations for show off and do not bother to check the actual use of their donation. It is crucial to replace rajas by sattva as the dominant guna, because if rajasik cravings are not controlled, they make a person perform even tamasik acts.

The type of thoughts entertained during our lifetime determine the type of impressions we will retain after departure from the current physical structure. One retains the qualities of the mode of nature which has been dominant during the previous life time. Guna dominant at the time of death, however, does affect the type of life one will have in next birth. As per Gita, when a man dies during the predominance of sattva, he attains the pure worlds of the pious. He, whose conduct has been good throughout his life and who has performed good actions, but dies when rajas is dominant, he is born as a human being with good conduct and emotions and performs good actions.

When one has lived with the dominance of the mode of passion in his life, he is born as a human amongst those attached to action. When one dies in the preponderance of the mode of ignorance or tamas, he is born in the wombs of the deluded, including creatures such as beasts, birds, moths, insects, trees, creepers etc. If a person performs good actions but at the time of death, he has a predominance of the mode of ignorance and is born in the womb of deluded one, then too he maintains his virtues, good conduct, and nature.

Actions performed by sattvik, rajas and tamas doers are called sattvik, rajas and tamas actions respectively because the guna of the doer is reflected in the activity. It is difficult to discipline the mind to change the dominant guna but with practice one can change the type of actions and become a doer with different dominant guna. Changing the type of actions and disciplining our external activities is relatively easy as compared to disciplining the mind. When noble action is undertaken it soon becomes a habit and this external habit of discipline tends to discipline the mind.

3

ATTACHMENT, DETACHMENT AND AVERSION

II Attachment is the great fabricator of illusions. Reality can be attained only by someone who is detached.... Simone Weil II

Contemplating constantly on the objects of senses, a man develops attachment for them. Due to this attachment he begins to enjoy these sense-objects either physically or in the mind.

The pleasure resulting from enjoyment further enhances attachment. From attachment springs desire. After fulfilling a desire, one desires for more. To desire for more after the current desire is fulfilled, is 'greed'. Excess of greed is called 'thirst'. Obstruction to fulfilment of greed by a stronger person generates fear while the obstruction from a weaker person arouses anger. Anger gives rise to delusion. It is delusion which makes us believe that ego is important for our existence. Delusion can also occur due to attachment and desire. Delusion from desire makes us want favourable sense objects and events in the future. Man begins to perform undesirable actions. He cannot distinguish between right and wrong and he is willing to cheat others by using fraudulent means. As a result of desire, greed and attachment a man thinks of his own selfish motive and pleasure while in anger he even thinks of harming others. To rid ourselves of these harmful aspects, we should first renunciate attachment and then desire, greed etc. With the renunciation of attachment, it will be easier to relinquish the rest.

Most people, however, are the servants of the senses and their life is controlled by them. Their senses function loosely and without any restriction. The test of a striver is that he should be able to control his senses whenever he wants to. The tortoise withdraws its six limbs, four legs, tail and the head, to protect itself from any danger. Similarly, a striver should also withdraw his five senses and the mind as soon as he sees any signs of attachment and aversion. By thus nipping the desire and anger in the bud, one can easily keep himself safe.

A subtle explanation of attachment and detachment is given in this story from 'The Speaking Tree'. A guru accompanied by his disciple went for a walk by the seashore. Both had embraced monkhood. They noticed a young pretty girl was drowning and shouting

for help. Sensing the impending danger, the guru dropped his water pot and ran towards the drowning girl, picked her up and brought her ashore to safety. The guru helped her out and spent a few minutes to comfort her till she regained consciousness. Thereafter the guru and the disciple continued walking. They walked for long time in silence. The disciple then asked, 'Guruji, we practice strict code of monkhood and detachment but you were touching the girl to save her even though you are forbidden to be in company of a female'. Guru replied, 'I picked her up, saved her and soon after removed her thought from my mind. I was detached thereafter. You did not touch her or save her, but you are still attached to the idea that I had picked her up, not just at that moment but for so many hours in your mind". You can decide who was attached and who was detached.

Most of the people find it difficult to get rid of attachment despite knowing well that they have to leave this world one day leaving

everything behind. Man came with nothing and will go away empty handed. After the carnage in Kurukshetra, Dhritrashtra wondered what the purpose of life was. Vidura, then, tells him the story of the man in the jungle running from wild beasts who falls in a pit. Creepers break his fall; but as he dangles there, he sees a large snake waiting at the bottom of the pit. The beasts prowl above. Black and white mice nibble at the roots of the creepers holding him. Bees fly from the side of the pit to sting him, but from their hive drops of honey fall. Almost without thinking, he reaches a finger out to taste the honey. The honey is incredibly sweet and despite facing certain death in all directions, the man can only think of how it tastes and desires more. In Vidura's interpretation, the jungle is our danger filled world, the serpent is time which waits for us all. The black and white mice are the nights and days that eat away the creepers of our life's journey. The honey is the pleasure that we get from this world and the intense desire to live and attachment to the pleasure keeps us dangling despite the sure death that we all face.

When we begin to have attachment or aversion to a sense object, we hold the sense object responsible for these feelings. But, in fact, attachment and aversion do not reside in the sense objects. The sense-objects, by themselves, are incapable of bringing any wave of sorrow or agitation. If they did, the same objects might have been desirable or undesirable equally to everyone. But it does not happen. Rain is desirable for a farmer but not so for a potter. Moreover, the same object is sometimes pleasant to a person while it is unpleasant at other times to the same person. Cool air is pleasant in summer but unpleasant in winter. Each sense has its own attraction for a pleasant aspect and aversion for an unpleasant one. The mind gets disturbed because when stimuli reach the mind it accepts certain types of stimuli as good and their opposites as bad. Thereafter it gets attached to the stimuli it experiences as good and develops aversion for the opposite type of stimuli. Attachment and aversion also seem to abide in the intellect because of which one's own beliefs appear pleasant and beliefs of others unpleasant. Attachment and aversion abide neither exclusively in inert nor in conscious state. These live only in the assumed relation between the inert and the conscious. Attraction for the insentient (matter) is attachment. When actions are performed out of attachment and aversion, the attachment and aversion are strengthened. Even the non-performance of actions due to attachment and aversion, further strengthens attachment and aversion.

It is possible to categorise attachment into three categories. Attachment which is devoid of any selfish motive, like that of a mother for her child, can be called Sattvik. Purity of this attachment goes away as soon as desire to achieve everything for the child

at any cost arises or expectations from the child become the motive. In the first case it reeks of selfishness and in the second case it becomes a transaction. Attachment to a sense object containing self-interest can be categorised as Rajasik. Such attachment is harmless for others if someone does not become a hinderance in getting what the person desires. A determined rajasik person will do anything to fulfil his attachment related desires. He will also take all measures to avoid situations that he dislikes. Rajasik persons consider fulfilment of desires related to senses as eternal happiness while it is merely a temporary pleasure. Most of the rajasik persons attend various spiritual discourses sincerely but forget to apply on themselves due to preference to worldly pleasures Tamasik attachment is full of lust, infatuation, greed and craving for something at the cost of others.

A striver should be so even minded while performing actions that he should not bother about their accomplishment or non-accomplishment. He should put in the best effort towards accomplishment but should not be concerned about the outcome. If we practice evenness of mind, we will soon achieve equanimity and detachment. We must understand that nothing belongs to us. No worldly object is personal. It belongs to the world. The world is almost a well-endowed guest house. Nature meets all our wants. All tasks are achieved with actions of many and with the resources already available in the world. We are only allowed to do the effort but the human ownership is only notional and attachment only harms. Even if there is attachment of some kind, one must be prepared to get detached at a moment's notice. The secret is to be attached outwardly but remain detached inwardly, i.e. attachment with detachment.

There are several forces of attraction and repulsion in the nature. Plants and animals are drawn to food and they are alert to threats. Humans cling to possessions that grant them value in society. We convince ourselves that our social status defines our identity. A man is in grief when he classifies objects and persons into two divisions – my own and not my own, of my caste and not of my caste, my follower and not my follower etc. Because of this, the faults such as grief, worry fear, commotion, and strain etc, arise.

When we sleep, we forget all external contacts. We regain freshness, vitality, and health which we are unable to get in the wakeful state. Energy is gained through mental dissociation with objects. Mere staying away from the things in life is not the sign of detachment. Many people desert their duties in life and run away, thinking that since they have developed perfect detachment from the sensuous world, they will gain their goal in the quietude of jungle or in the solitude of mountains. Physical abandonment of house, property or other possessions is not detachment if one continues

to attach importance to them in the heart or if he feels proud that he is a renouncer. It only implies that the attachment continues. This disturbance does not depend upon the presence or the absence of the sense-objects. If the mind's agitations for procuring the desirable objects, or for getting rid of the undesirable ones remain detachment will never be complete.

Mind must attach itself to something. Mind, if not controlled, will always respond to whatever stimuli is sent by the senses. Senses do not, by themselves, decide on likes and dislikes. Mind does that, based on the impressions that are formed over the lifetime and before. Its attachment and aversion to likes and dislikes dictate its instructions to the sense organs for appropriate action. Mind plays very important role in our journey to achieve detachment. Even though mind is the most important element of all action, we should practice to make it behave like the lotus leaf. Though the lotus leaf exists only in

water, draws its nourishment from the water and dies away in the same water, yet during its life as a leaf, it does not allow itself to be moistened by water.

A sick man is unable to indulge due to sickness but craving for sense enjoyment persists. He may dislike the taste of everything but he hopes to enjoy these after every recovery. In some cases that becomes the driving motivation to follow the hard treatment regime very sincerely. Similarly, abstinence may enable one to restrain body and senses but mind may still wander. Mahatma Gandhi recommends fasting as a tool to control attachment and desire but with a caution, "The Shastras say that if a man's appetite is not under his control, it is best for him to fast. The appetite subsides but our pleasure in the objects of senses remains. During a fast, impure desires will probably subside, but one gets impatient for the fast to end. Unless the desire disappears completely, the fast will not endure". The fasting that he recommends is not essentially for food. It can be for anything that one craves for and on which one has become dependent due to avoidable attachment.

4

INTELLECT

II Intellect is the ability to keep the mind balanced and its agility under control. II

Intellect is the logical side of the human mind. It refers to the cognition and rational mental processes gained through external input rather than internal. All perceptions are received through the sense organs in the raw form. This information, however, needs to be processed before any action is initiated by the organs of action. It is, therefore, conveyed to the mind which, in turn, conveys it to intellect for vetting. Intellect takes the final logical decision based on the inputs and pre-stored impressions and memories, and passes it back to the mind. Mind, then, issues necessary instructions to the organs of action which, in turn, execute the necessary response. Each such transaction leaves a new impression or memory in the mind-intellect equipment to act as an input for future decisions. For maximum efficiency, the team of sense organs, mind and intellect must act in perfect coordination.

Gita lays a lot of importance on developing the intellect. Mind is very agile and can make a person drift in a flash. Intellect is important to keep mind in check and help mind in taking right decisions. Most people don't understand the importance of intellect and the need to strengthen it. They, therefore make choices with weak intellect. Mind is the seat of emotion, impulse and like and dislike. Intellect discriminates, judges, discerns, weighs the pros and cons and arrives at a decision. Mind is irrational, intellect is rational. Aim should be to make mind work for you and not against you. A mind not governed by intellect is dangerous because it can distract, trick and mislead you.

Comprehension is done at four levels, namely physical. mental, intellectual, and spiritual level. Each level enables us to appreciate the same object or same situation differently. When physically we see a person, we may mentally identify that person to be a relative, friend or foe. At intellectual level we will say that it is merely a bundle of bone and flesh made of five elements, i.e. water, earth, air, fire and ether and it experiences change constantly. At spiritual level, we would identify that person as temporary abode of the embodied soul. If we function at intellectual and spiritual levels, it becomes easier to detach ourselves from the worldly objects.

Three types of intellects have been defined in eighteenth chapter of Gita. Sattvik intellect

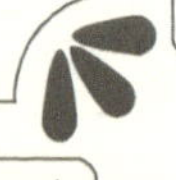

is the intellect which knows the path of action and renunciation. If a man has a desire, it becomes a bondage whether he possesses the desired thing or not. But if he is free from desire, he is liberated whether he possesses the thing or not. Thus, the intellect is sattvik if it knows the reality about the path of work and renunciation and also what ought to be done and what ought not to be done. On the other hand, rajasik intellect understands dharma and adharma wrongly. Because of attachment the rajasik intellect possesses evil propensities, such as selfishness, partiality and inequanimity etc. It makes the person perform actions accordingly and does not let him achieve freedom from bondage. Tamasik intellect perceives wrong as right and is enveloped in darkness all the time. Tamasik intellect hankers after mundane pleasures, considering them as real and looks upon vices as virtues.

Intellect of those whose aim is to enjoy worldly pleasure is indiscriminate while the intellect of those with aim of equanimity, is discriminate. The discriminative intellect is full of conviction and is steady and resolute. When a man discards all his desires visiting the mind and is satisfied in own self, he is said to be stable in wisdom. With regard to indiscriminate intellect, Mahatma Gandhi has said, "Persons filled with endless desires; individuals who are ever thinking of heaven; men who persuade people to perform innumerable rituals to secure enjoyment and win greatness, persons who advise us to propitiate a great many gods and so make us feel helpless; men who induce us to offer fanciful prayers to imaginary gods and turn us away from prayer to the God of all gods – such individuals push us deeper and deeper into quagmire".

Due to attachment the Self considers that the multiple and unlimited desires are in itself, while actually they are not.

Due to this belief by Self, the intellect does not remain steady. The intellect of the person who is free from desires remains content automatically. Generally, people endeavour to calm the mind to make it steady. For this they practice hard. Gita, however gives importance to stability of intellect and not to stability of mind. A steady mind will not allow adventure, curiosity, innovation, and exploration etc and will limit growth and evolution. The external activities will come to a halt if the mind becomes stable. A steady mind and a mind out of control are both not desirable. Mind needs to be calm and under control. An active mind controlled by a steady intellect will be the best option for growth. We, therefore, need to make our intellect steady. A person having equanimity has intellect which remains steadfast and is never caught in a whirlpool. A striver with steadfast wisdom may externally seem to relate to people, objects etc but he is totally dissociated from inside. It is, however, not

necessary that a man will become of steady wisdom if he can disconnect his sense organs from pleasure but it is certain that if a man attains steady wisdom, his sense organs will automatically come under his control.

5

ACTION AND THE DOER

II All actions are performed by modes of nature. He whose mind is disillusioned by egoism thinks, "I am the doer" ..... Gita 3:27 II

It is generally considered that an action involves physical movement of the body. We only consider the acts of walking, climbing, cooking etc as actions. So, when we are not involved in any of these, we say that no action is being performed. Thus, sitting idle would imply that the person is not involved in any action. The activities by subtle and causal body are also action. When we are thinking intensely, we are invariably physically quiet and inactive. In the physical inactivity, there is intense activity going on deep within. We can see the actions by the five organs of action, because they receive inputs from the five sense organs. These sense organs are controlled by mind and intellect and the activities of mind and intellect are not visible. Therefore, actions performed by the physical body, subtle body and by the causal body, are all actions of the body. We are performing action all the time whether we are involved in any visible activity or not. Nature is active all the time and therefore, as part of the nature, the body is also active all the time. It is a misnomer to say that we would be free from all action if we withdraw from society and isolate ourselves and if there is no action, there would also be no fruit of action. By simply withdrawing from society, we do not get freedom from action. So long as the physical body is alive, some activities like breathing, digesting etc, always go on and mind and intellect continue to work.

It is fear which drives everyone to action. Fear can be of many types. Fear can be of survival, reputation, competition etc. Some fear may be real but most of it is imaginary. Having satisfied the hunger today, man wants to hoard for future due to the fear that the supplies might finish. He consumes medicines for fear of death. He wants himself to be remembered and therefore works hard to create a legacy. For all these he continues to perform action and uses all possible means to survive. Soul cannot be destroyed or harmed and does not need to do anything for its survival. It also develops fear of death, which has no meaning for soul, but, due to attachment with the body and the material world it begins to crave for action and accordingly forces action through the mind. One action leads to another and the chain never ends. Each of these actions results in fruit. If one action does not give him the desired result, he does another and thus continues to look for ways to win over his fears. The uncertainties of life enhance the fear further and man tries to control things on which he has absolutely no control. Man also passes on his fears to the next generation which does the same to their next one and it goes on.

Humans possess ability of discrimination and imagination; which does not exist in other life forms. Judicious use of the ability to discriminate maintains us on the right path, keeps our life purposeful and leads to success in all our efforts. Immature imagination, emanating from fear, can lead to wasteful action. It can also cause stress and more fear. One may end up setting targets which do not exist or are impractical. If we imagine good things for ourselves, we start working to consolidate them and if we imagine misfortune, we start taking steps to thwart them. No one knows when and in what manner the fruits of our actions will appear. We speculate and start performing new actions and bind ourselves for no reason.

Depending on the motive with which they are performed, actions can be divided into three categories: activity, action and inaction. Initially, each action is *kriya* or activity. An activity undertaken according to spiritual prescriptions but with a desire for fruit, is called action or *karma*. Activity performed for the welfare of others without desire for fruit and attachment is classified as inaction or *akarma*. Physical abandonment of action is not inaction. When the person has the egoistic notion that he is the doer of an action, his action becomes karma, which bears fruit. But when he has no notion of doership, his action remains a mere activity, does not turn into karma and does not bear fruit. When a man has desire, actions are performed but when the desire is enhanced or aggravated, forbidden actions also get performed.

We should not stop performing an activity just because there is a fear of an unfavourable outcome. Result and fruit are not in our hands. We can have control over our actions, but we have no control over others' actions. Others' actions also influence the result, directly or indirectly. A man continues to perform activity throughout his life time and due to dominance of rajas guna, most of it results in karma or fruit-earning actions. We can only ensure the action to be within the spiritual parameters, as per our knowledge and interpretation. We cannot judge whether an action will result in punishment or reward. Everyone would like to just go on receiving rewards but enjoying reward also earns fruit, for which one has to go through another lifetime. It results in more karma, loaded with more fruit and the cycle goes on. A man has to take birth either to be free of obligations or receive these from others for previous births. He cannot get rid of the cycle of death and birth so long as he does not repay his debt or receive his dues. The way to close this account is that he should pay to others what he owes to them and should not expect them to repay to him. In both situations the striver should be detached.

It is futile to blame ourselves for being victims of any of nature's tragic events. At times, these even shake up our faith and we begin to wonder about existence of God or another higher force and its justice. When impacted by these events, we tend to wonder why such things have to happen only to us. We are conditioned by our judgmental evaluation of every situation as good or bad based on how it affects us. These events are not linked to goodness, integrity, faith, race or colour of their victims. They are not any punishment to the affected individuals. These are the fruit of our past actions, appearing as circumstances. It is upto us how we react in those circumstances.

It is we who call the circumstances favourable or unfavourable. Just by themselves the circumstances cannot make a person happy or sad unless one starts identifying himself with them. Our right is only to perform our duty, but never to claim its fruit. It does not imply that the fruit of action is to be renounced; it is the desire for fruit of action which must be renounced. It is not possible for anyone to renounce fruit of action because fruit is not in anyone's hands. Renouncement of fruit of action will be when a striver does not desire the visible or even unreceived fruit, nor does he feel pleased or displeased having received it. We do not have right to claim fruit of action because all actions are performed with the help of worldly objects and other persons. No action can be performed alone by anyone. When we eat food, we should not forget the large number of persons and agencies involved from the stage when seed was first sown.

Each action involves many people at different stages. It is, sheer dishonesty to desire the fruit of actions for only own self.

Thoughts play an important part in leading a person to action. Action comes from desire emerging from thoughts. Thoughts come from impressions that we gather and are influenced by inborn urge or deep-rooted inclination. Impressions consolidate as desire and manifest as action. If you think of a negative thought, you become more evil. On the contrary, emergence of a positive, loving, elevating thought leads to happiness and spiritual growth. It is upto us to use our free will for our evolution.

The three constituents of action are the agent or *karta*, the action and instruments. There are thirteen instruments, both external and internal, which help us in performing an action. Five organs of action, i.e. hand, foot, mouth (organ of voice), anus and genital organ and five sense organs i.e. ear, eye,

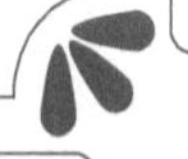

skin, tongue and nose constitute the external instruments of senses. Mind, intellect, and egoism are the internal instruments. Besides these thirteen, the impressions are the motivators or the force that drives one to act and decide the way one will act. With these impressions everyone develops his own definition of right and wrong. These impressions urge him to act in a particular way and define the person's preferences. The action which he prefers, books which he reads, work which he enjoys, work which he does not enjoy etc, are all governed by the impressions. The accumulated impressions determine texture of thoughts. Texture of thoughts differentiates one man's personality from the personality of another. These textures compel deep urges in us that determine our emotional profile and emotional response at any given time. It is, therefore, very important that one chooses environment of positivity and rationalises his impressions intelligently.

People in this world are attached to action. It is because of their attachment to action that they are charmed by success which is attained through action and feel sad when things do not work out the way they have desired. God does not decree what type of actions a person will have to perform. Had it been so, man would not have to bear fruit of his actions because actions have been predetermined by Lord Himself. At every stage of the action this world of duality provides options to everyone to choose from and one has to take responsibility for the choice made.

The movement of mind, intellect, and the account of all our actions and impressions from one body to another, is called death of the former body and birth of the latter. At birth, distinct traits and ambitions appear from nowhere. These are the reflections of what you carried from the previous birth. The sum of all your karmas till date is called *sanchit* or accumulated karma. Of these a

few powerful ones that exert pressure for fulfillment are called *prarabdh* or destined karma. They determine your birth in an environment that is tailor made for their exhaustion. During our lifetime fruits of our past actions will be provided, irrespective of what we do. They will appear in our life as circumstances and we would have no control over them. It is upto us to call them pleasant or unpleasant, reward or punishment but by doing so we accumulate more karma. We can avoid that by being equanimous while those circumstances last.

Kriyaman are the actions of the present. These bear fruit in two forms – direct fruit and indirect fruit. Indirect fruit is received in the form of impressions or sanskar. Direct fruit is of two kinds – seen and unseen. The seen fruit can further be divided into two – immediate and remote. For example, the immediate fruit of the tasteful food is that it satisfies hunger and its fruit in future is that it gives strength. Similarly, he who eats excess chilli gets burning sensation as the immediate fruit. Its future fruit will be the disease that the excess chilli would cause. Acts of sacrifice, gift, penance, pilgrimage and chanting etc may bear seen fruit here in the form of riches, praise, and honour etc, and unseen fruit hereafter in the attainment of heaven (as is the belief). Similarly, fruit of evil actions can lead to fine, imprisonment etc as the seen fruit, which may be reaped here while birth in lower forms of life and stay in hell (as per the belief) is the unseen fruit which may be reaped hereafter.

All actions which are in accordance with the scriptures and performed without attachment or aversion, where no reward is sought and where the performer abandons doership or ego, once the action is completed – are sattvik in nature. Doership should remain only during the performance of the action and once the action is over, the doership should dissolve and one should shift focus to other actions which need attention. If action is performed for fruit and is pushed by egoism, it is rajasik in nature. Rajasik actions are performed to seek comfort, pleasure, honour, praise and gratification etc. Rajasik person feels happy when people praise him in public. In private, he feels proud by thinking that he is more efficient, sincere, and honest in actions than the other people. If action is performed out of delusion and without regard to its consequences – it is considered tamasik in nature. While performing action a tamasik person does not consider whether he possesses the requisite ability, time, skill, knowledge and has required resources or not. It is possible that, depending upon the manner and the intent with which it is performed, any action can get classified as sattvik, rajasik or tamasik.

Similarly, the doer or *karta* can also be of three types. A sattvik karta is free from attachment and does not possess ego. He is endowed with firmness and zeal and remains equanimous in success and failure. The

sattvik karta works in a spirit of sacrifice for a higher ideal. On the other hand, a rajasik karta is passionate and eagerly seeks the fruit of action. He is greedy and is easily moved by joy and sorrow. He offers charity to gain honour and praise and is never satisfied with his possessions. The rajasik karta acts for selfish ends but the result is stress and mental agitation. Tamasik karta is arrogant and he cannot discriminate between the proper and the improper, remains unbending and is hard hearted by nature, having no humility. Out of delusion he holds that his own ideas are good and sticks to them. Mahatma Gandhi has said – 'You should shed your attachment to ego and work – that is work with the thought that you are not the doer of karma and its fruit is not meant for you to enjoy. You should act as if you were a piece of inert matter like the spindle of the spinning wheel or like the wick of a lamp which goes on burning by itself'. Swami Prabhupada in his commentary

'Bhagvad Gita As It Is' has written, "To revel in ego and hope is an attempt on our part to live either with the dead moments of the past or with the unborn moments of the future. The renunciation of action also means giving up of the wrong motives behind the actions. It is usually believed that right action itself will take us to the Infinite. This is impossible. An action itself is a child of desire". Abandoning an action out of fear of physical suffering and pain, is rajasik tyag and relinquishing work due to ignorance, indolence and heedlessness is tamasik tyag. Both kinds of relinquishments must be totally avoided.

All the resources to sustain our body are available in the world before we are born and they would remain after we are gone. We are merely visitors who keep visiting and revisiting. We use world's resources, including our body, for our own pleasure and prosperity. The world does not belong to us. We are, therefore indebted to the world.

We can repay our debt by performing our duty towards the world i.e. for the welfare of others. While the word 'others' implies all the other beings, we should not forget that our own bodies are also included in 'others'. These bodies are the gross, subtle, and causal bodies. The service to the gross body is in not allowing it to be lazy, sleepy, lax etc. Not allowing them to enjoy worldly pleasures would be service to organs of senses and organs of action. The service to mind is in not allowing it to think evil and not engage in wasteful thoughts.

Destiny influences intellect. It can compel a person to take right or wrong decisions to support the situation that the destiny wants to create as fruit of his past actions. Being guided by his intellect a businessman may make profit or loss. This gain or loss is decided by destiny and the man may not have any control over it. But the man is free to have honest or dishonest dealings. If a man dies of natural causes, accidents etc for

reasons beyond his control, it is predestined. If, however, a man commits suicide, it is untimely death and he, who commits suicide, incurs the sin of murder. Similarly, take the case of a criminal who is sentenced to be hanged for his crime. Now, another person kills this criminal before his sentence is carried out. The killer of the criminal will surely be tried for murder, and will be punished for the same because the criminal might still be having legal remedies left to fight for his life but the murderer has ended that possibility. A man can be free from fruits of virtuous actions by surrendering them to God without any desire for fruit, but it is not possible to get rid of sins in this manner. Sins being the actions against the scriptures, cannot be surrendered to Lord. One will have to suffer the fruit of sins. Once a sinful action has been performed and the doer has realised it, he attempts to offset it by virtuous actions like going to temple, making a donation etc.

It is all wasteful because the sins cannot be counteracted by virtuous actions. The two are accumulated separately. But if one performs any good act in order to repent his wrongdoing, his sins perish.

6

KARMYOG

II Your right is only to perform your duty, but never to claim its fruit ... Gita 2:47 II

Karmyog is to undertake whatever scriptures approved duty comes in front of us as per stage of life, nature or circumstances and to perform it without having any desire, affection or attachment to its fruits and by maintaining equanimity whether one is successful or not. What happens on its own, in the nature, is called activity. Gradual transition of our body from childhood to old age is an activity. Breathing is an activity. No one can be blamed or credited with what happens during an activity. Flow of a river is an activity. If someone drowns in its water and dies or someone has good crop because of its water, no blame or benefit goes to the river. It is only when we attach ourselves to the activity due to desire, the activity becomes an action. Man becomes a doer and earns its fruit.

All of us want only the favourable circumstances and will do anything to prolong them. Similarly, unfavourable circumstances are disliked and we make all efforts to avoid them or to ensure that they are over soon. We credit ourselves for the favourable circumstances and make use of those for ourselves alone and blame others for the unfavourable ones. This is, perhaps, due to rajasik guna being so dominant in the society. While enjoying as well as cursing, we forget that we are binding ourselves more and more and that this would become cause

for more fruits in future. Circumstances are meant to exhaust the fruit of our past karmas, and they should not be used to enhance our karma burden. By enjoying or suffering the circumstances, we are only piling up new karma. After satisfying our need, and not greed, we should be humble and use the favourable circumstances to serve the needy and the destitute. Similarly, in the unfavourable circumstances we should be patient and thank Lord for destroying our past sins. We should only focus on the activity. We should learn to accept whatever result or fruit we get for our actions, as God's will. If we get favourable fruit, we must remember that many people are responsible for our success. We should share favourable fruit with others. Unfavourable fruits should be taken as learning opportunity and we should identify our shortcomings and urge ourselves to work harder.

Senses are superior to objects of senses. It means that the senses know the objects but objects do not know the senses. Senses can live without objects but without senses the existence of objects cannot be established. Every sense knows its own objects but does not know the objects of other senses. Ears can only perceive sound, tongue only taste, nose can only smell, eyes can only see and skin can only perceive touch. But the mind knows the five senses and their objects. Therefore, the mind is superior, more powerful, more subtle and has wider range of activity than senses. The intellect knows whether the mind is quiet or turbulent and whether senses function properly or not. It means the intellect knows the mind and its thoughts, as well as senses and their objects. Therefore, intellect is greater, more powerful, more subtle and has a wider range of activity than the mind. When Self attaches itself to the body, it is called 'ego'. The master of intellect is ego, and due to the assumed attachment with the body 'ego' becomes the doer.

Most of the time whatever action we perform, we do it with a purpose. This way we attach ourselves to that action. We go to temple to request a specific fruit. To get our desire fulfilled, we do not even hesitate to bargain with Lord by offering a deal of certain donation, conduct of certain pooja, observance of fasts etc. Our right is only to perform our duty and never to claim its fruit. In Kurukshetra, Lord told Arjun, "Your domain is only to lift the bow and arrow, aim at the target and shoot the arrow. I will decide whether your arrow will hit the target or not and whether your enemy will fall or not. You only perform your part and leave the rest to me". Same applies to all of us in our daily life.

Desire is the root cause of all sins. First desire attracts the senses towards the objects, then the senses attract the mind. The senses and mind attract the intellect. Identifying with the intellect, the embodied soul prefers to re-live the remembered experiences of sense-enjoyments and mental joys. Thus, desire deludes the embodied soul and drives it to ruin. When desire is not satisfied it gives rise to anger. From anger arises delusion which destroys discrimination. We stop doing what ought to be done and do what ought not to be done. When a desire is satisfied, it gives birth to greed, leading to more desires.

We find ourselves unable to let go of the desires because we convince ourselves that we can't grow if we stop desiring. We consider that desire is necessary for all action and it is, therefore, not possible to renounce desires. It is impossible to satisfy all desires. While awake, we feel happy and sad because of our affinity with sense-objects. During sleep also this attachment lingers and gives us disturbed sleep. But during sound sleep we do not remember sense-objects at all and we feel very fresh when we wake up. Thus, it is the renunciation of sense-objects which provides us joy and peace.

When we perform a wrong action and we get an immediate fruit in the form of an injury, loss, sickness or punishment by law, we immediately blame the destiny. We forget that at every stage and every situation, we have choices and we have full freedom to choose one. A thief's son does not have to become a thief. He can select a different path for himself. Destiny only encourages us to action but never compels anyone to perform prohibited actions. Destiny only wants to improve us constantly.

All actions will bear fruit. The worldly things can be enjoyed externally by the organs as well as internally by the mind. Enjoyment in mind is very harmful because one gets opportunity to enjoy without any fear of anyone coming to know. A person goes on enjoying these with his mind and develops a false pride that he has renounced pleasures. Enjoyment in mind also helps the person to sustain his good image in public. Such a person is called a hypocrite. He, however

forgets that all is being recorded in the mind-intellect equipment for appropriate fruit in future.

The three types of gunas define nature and thinking of a man. This defines the type of desires one will have and the impact these will have on individual discrimination. Sattvik desires are like fire which illuminates with bright flames. The smoke may cover the fire and apparently affect its brightness, but the intensity of the flame is not affected. The sattvik desires cover the soul but the soul remains as glorious as ever. Rajasik desires cause agitations in the minds of a person because of his unrelenting quest for glory and power. Veiling of the intellect, caused by these agitations is strong. This veiling caused by the rajasik desires can be compared with dust on a mirror. Dust on a mirror can be cleaned only by our own efforts. It cannot be blown away. Through the smoke, however thick it might be, the fire can be perceived; but through the dust, only a dim reflection

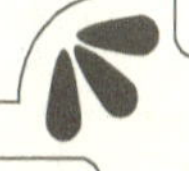

can be seen in the mirror. Tamasik desires completely cover intellect and diviner aspects of one's personality. Mind and intellect get deluded. Person with tamasik guna fails to even notice the delusion. Such veiling continues to remain till the tamasik person evolves himself and is able to win over this nature and guna.

One first tries the legitimate means to get the desired object. If he is not successful, he will go to any length and use any method to get it. Having achieved it, he starts working on getting another, and it goes on. All the desires, however, do not lead to ruin. Desire can be for spiritual purpose or for worldly purposes. The spiritual desires are not really desires. The desire for self- realisation and the desire to render selfless service to others, are not desires. The desire to utilise resources in rendering service to the world is renunciation and not desire. Desire for food for sustenance is a necessity for the body, rather than a desire.

The worldly desire is never satisfied. By enjoying the object of desire; it is rather strengthened. Fulfilment of desire leads to greed. When a man gets a hundred rupees, he desires to earn a thousand rupees. He feels that he needs nine hundred more and he desires to work towards getting them. When he earns thousand rupees, he desires to have ten thousand rupees. Now he desires nine thousand more. And it goes on. The richer he grows greedier he becomes. It is not the money or his need which drives him, but the desire and greed.

We should see everyone with equal eye so that we are impartial and dispassionate, i.e.'*samdarshi*. We should behold the Lord pervading everywhere and should love all beings and think of their welfare equally without attachment, aversion, pride, partiality etc. In day-to-day life, our dealings with all beings are however, not same. Being '*samvarti*' with equal dealings with everyone is neither proper nor possible. A gold statue

of God and that of a dog will cost the same if they are of the same weight and the gold used is identical. But we worship the divine statue but look down on the statue of the dog even though both are made of gold. The best examples of not being *samvarti* come from our dealings with our own body parts. We see all the parts of our body with an equal eye and think of their welfare equally, but our dealings with them are different. When our feet touch someone, we feel sorry and apologise but we do not do so when our arm touches someone. We show our reverence for others by bowing our heads and folding our hands rather than using our feet. When our hand touches our own foot, we need to wash the hand. However, to show our reverence and respect, we touch elders' feet and instead of washing hands, we touch our forehead or our heart as a mark of respect.

Happiness and sorrow are two sides of the same coin. None of these stays forever. We should prepare ourselves for both as none of them can be permanent. They will keep appearing as our response to various circumstances that occur in our life. Happiness looks good when coming and bad when going away. Similarly, grief looks bad when coming and looks good when going away. How can, then, we say which one is better than the other? We should treat them equally, and with equanimity. Same applies to other sets of dualities, like pleasure and pain, loss and gain etc. Equanimity means maintaining equilibrium in the circumstances created by the pairs of opposites. If a person has equanimity in all dualities, he would rarely be tempted to incur sinful acts. Nothing in the world is wholly good or wholly evil Where there will be crests, there will also be troughs. How will a crest be known if there is no trough? In every situation, we should expect both.

If it is not easy to avoid accumulating karma, we must find the right way to live with karma. We should ourselves be accountable for our actions and their impact. We should not outsource the responsibility to parents, teachers, politicians, country, gods and fate and take full responsibility of shaping our destiny with our own hands. We do get influenced by our environment, circumstances and impressions but we need to take charge of our lives. What befalls us may be the consequence of collective karma but we should realise that we are an individual even if we are part of a family, group or a crowd. It is we who will get the fruits of our individual actions. If we overeat, it is we who would get indigestion. When we fall sick, we will not get well if someone else decides to take medicines on our behalf. Enlightenment can only happen to an individual. The problem is that karmik memory is part of us and when we are deeply identified with this memory, our perception becomes seriously clouded. This is when karma becomes a limitation. We may identify with worldly definitions of family, clan, tribe, class, gender, religion, culture and language, but slowly these definitions start influencing our judgements and decisions.

Another and most effective way of living with karma is, becoming a mere observer to all the action that the body performs. As part of the Supersoul, you are not the body and therefore you should not associate yourself with what the body does. This association results in doership and when we let go of the doership, peace dawns and we experience happiness and stability. By disconnecting from the body, which includes the mind, we become a mere onlooker in every event. Imagine every situation as a triangle where one corner is the body, the second corner is the mind and the third corner is you, as an onlooker. You merely watch mind and body interact and perform all action, without identifying with what is happening. Be like the steam of an engine which is neither appreciated nor blamed if the train reaches early or late or whether the train goes to right destination or not. If the body receives

an injury, do not think that you are injured. You only identify that there is an injury to the body. This detaching from the body can only be achieved with lot of practice but, once achieved, it is the best way to deal with karma of the body, where no fruit is earned. This detachment is neither helplessness nor inability. The events of joy and sorrow come to everyone, but a karmyogi knows them as the fruits of past deeds and stays unaffected. He does not begin a new cycle of karma; he exhausts the old stock with equanimity.

7

GYANYOG AND BHAKTIYOG

II The unreal has no existence and the real never ceases to be ….. Gita 2:16 II

II Those who, fixing their mind on Me, worship Me ever steadfast and are endowed with supreme faith, are the most perfect yogis… Gita 12/2 II

Path of devotion, also known as *Gyan Yog*, *Gyan Marg* or *Sankhyayog*, is one of the several spiritual paths that pursue knowledge of the truth. Gyan, or knowledge, refers to any cognitive event that is correct and true over time. It particularly refers to knowledge about reality of the Supreme Being. Gyan Yog aims at the realisation of the oneness of the individual self or soul and the ultimate Self, the Lord. In the Bhagavad Gita, *Gyan Yog* is also referred to as *Buddhi Yog* and its goal is self-realization. The Supreme Lord is the material cause of the creation which includes the lower nature (matter) and the higher nature (soul) of the Lord. Earth, water, fire, air, ether, mind, intellect, ego constitute Lord's lower nature. The life element, *Jeev*, by which this nature is sustained is His higher nature. Everything in the world is nothing but the manifestation of the Lord. The soul is eternal, omnipresent, immovable, constant and everlasting while the world is ever changing. Even though the soul is eternal, changeless and constant, it identifies itself with perishable matter and accepts the creation and dissolution of the matter as its own creation and dissolution. Since it accepts the activities of lower nature as its own or in other words attributes the doership to itself, it is called embodied soul, otherwise it is nothing else but God. The embodied soul being a portion of God cannot be proved to have its own separate existence independent of God as it is God itself. When it becomes free from the bondage of being a doer and an enjoyer, it is not higher nature or embodied soul any more. Whatever we can see, hear, touch, smell, understand is unreal because it changes continuously. That which never was cannot exist and that which exists cannot cease to exist. Everything which has a name and a form ceases one day to exist in that particular mode. Real is that which defies all changes and remains the same in all periods of time. This is the knowledge or *Gyan* and is the essence of Gyanyog.

Audio waves which emanate from a radio station travel in all directions but no one can hear them till they meet an instrument which can play the sound. It does not mean the waves do not exist where there is no such instrument. Similarly, consciousness is all pervading but it finds an expression whenever it meets a body which has a functional mind-body equipment. But, unlike the radio waves, consciousness is motionless. Take the case of a building which has space inside as well as outside it. In case the wall of the building collapses, the space inside simply merges with the space outside. There is no movement.

It is normally believed that the universe emanates from Him, abides in Him and also merges in Him. But Lord has stated in Gita that He does not abide in the universe. This may appear contradictory. But the fact is that if he has abode in the universe, he would have to decay and die as the universe decays and dies. This cannot happen. Lord also declares that the beings do not dwell in Him. The reason is that if beings had dwelt in Him, they would not have undergone any

change in them and they would not have perished. This also does not happen. Waves have no existence of their own, besides water, because waves are in water and water is in waves. As there is no independent existence of waves, there remains only water, which appears as waves. Similarly, the world has no existence of its own. It emanates from the Lord, appears to dwell in Him and merges in Him. The earthenware vessels are of nothing besides clay. So, it would appear there is clay in these vessels and they are in clay. But actually, it is not so. If there had been clay in earthenware vessels, with the destruction of the earthenware vessels the clay would also have been destroyed. But it does not happen. Similarly, if earthenware vessels had been in clay, they would remain safe for ever, like clay. But it is not so. It means that earthenware vessels are not in clay. In the same way neither does God dwell in the world nor does world dwell in God.

The winds move about everywhere in space; the space supports and envelops them everywhere, and yet they do not ever limit the space. When the wind is moving, the space does not move.

God cannot be called either existent or non-existent. As the Sun is different from both night and day so is God different from existent or non-existent. He exists, without and within all beings and constitutes the moving and also the unmoving creation. He is subtle, He is incomprehensible. He is undivided and yet He seems to be distributed over all beings. No wave is all the ocean, all the waves put together are also not the entire ocean. We cannot say that the ocean is attached to the waves since the ocean is the very nature of the waves and, though detached, all the waves are always supported by none other than the ocean itself. Cotton is in all cloth; cloth is not cotton. And yet it is the cotton in the cloth that supports the cloth.

We have all experienced that whenever the weather is cloudy and Sun is not visible, we say that the Sun has been covered by clouds. Actually, Sun is too big to be covered by any amount of cloud. It is we who, with our very limited span of visibility, conclude that the Sun is covered with the speck of cloud. We should remember that if we hold a finger close to our eyes, it blocks the view to even a mountain. It does not mean that the mountain does not exist anymore. Similar is our disconnect with the Supreme because, due to ignorance, the ego blocks our vision. Lord is always there; it is just that our ignorance and ego come in the way of realisation. When this ignorance is removed the Self becomes manifest just as when the cloud has moved away, the Sun becomes manifest.

Fuel is essential for running a vehicle. With fuel the same vehicle can take you to places, win a race for you or get crushed in an accident through over speeding or driving

error. It is the driver who achieves all these outcomes and the fuel cannot be credited or blamed. The fuel does not have any attachment with the driver who reaches his destination nor does it have any enmity with the person who meets with accident. With neither attachment nor hatred, the petrol gives us its power when invoked through the mechanism of the engine. Cooking gas can enable us to prepare delicious meals but it can also ruin our cooking, if we are not careful. Electricity can help us in running huge facilities to make our life easier. It can also electrocute a person. The vehicle fuel, cooking gas, electricity etc are available to power and energise our lives. But, use of the available power depends upon us and our wisdom in employing it. Similarly, the Lord lends His power to all without any partiality and it is up to the individuals how they utilise this unlimited power for their emancipation. Nature's resources and Lord's blessings are same for everyone but the man is free to make a choice.

The knowledge can be of three types. With sattvik knowledge one realises that the imperishable is present in all beings and is undivided, meaning that He is not separate in separate beings. This knowledge perceives the oneness underlying the universe. Rajasik knowledge, on the other hand, has predominance of passion. It is because of the attachment and aversion resulting from passion that a man sees diversity in different persons, gods, animals, trees etc, according to their shapes, forms and attributes etc. Even though he believes that God is one, yet driven by desire and attachment he does not hesitate in repeating his request to a number of god images and forms with the belief that at least one of them would get him what he desires. A man possessing rajasik knowledge is unable to discriminate between sentient and the insentient. A person with tamasik knowledge regards the perishable body as his own self. He identifies the soul with the body and is entangled in the mesh of delusion.

Path of knowledge is quite different from the path of devotion, or *Bhaktiyog*. Path of devotion is the path that the strivers follow for *bhaktiyog* or union with God through unconditional devotion to the Almighty. A bhaktiyogi sees God in every being and treats them accordingly. Whatever *bhaktiyogi* does is in the glory of God and is dedicated to Him. *Bhaktiyogi* has a pure heart which is full of love, kindness and care. He offers all his actions to God and seeks His mercy all the time. He does not desire anything for himself and always prays for the well-being of entire world.

There are two types of strivers on the path of devotion. One type of striver worships God as having a form as well as attributes. These strivers identify God as a human figure, or any living being or even an inert object having a shape. The shape helps them in concentrating and focussing. Representation of God and gods in human form is most popular because, being human themselves,

people can easily identify with them and relate to their life-story and glory. They can easily relate to them, emulate their actions and follow their examples and achievements. The idol, however, is only a symbol for an imperceptible and subtle Truth. To mistake the idol to be itself is to mistake the means for the end. And such a misunderstanding alone breeds fanatics, who sow seeds of rivalry and jealousy. The other type of strivers worship God which is shapeless and attributeless. It is comparatively more difficult to control a fickle mind and senses on the attributeless and formless Absolute. In this type of worship, it is necessary to not only control the senses fully but also the mind because so long as there is attachment of the mind with the sense objects, the Absolute cannot be attained. The worship of the attributeless God is rather dry in nature and due to this it becomes difficult to concentrate. The difficulty is greater for a striver who is attached to the body or the material objects. Such strivers come to know of their shortcomings late, and therefore, the required correction also gets delayed. A preceptor or guru, therefore becomes necessary for the spiritual journey of such striver.

People visit places of worship to seek fulfilment of their desires. They bargain and promise various things to the deity, if their selfish desire is fulfilled. Most of the people believe that all that they have to do is some fasting on specific days or promise some donation or promise some sacrifice. They don't even bother to see if the desire they hope to fulfil will harm others or not. They expect God to provide the demanded item manifold and, in the shape, and in manner which they had desired. Some people believe in conducting prayers involving large noisy crowds with the accompaniment of equally noisy instruments. They believe that more noise they make, easier it will be for the God to hear them and take notice.

In this game of show off they are not concerned about the discomfort they cause to the sick and elderly. They forget that prayer is a communication between the devotee and the Lord and it should be done as silently as possible.

There are two categories of prayers. The first category is the prayer for getting one or the other worldly desire fulfilled. Majority of the people praying belong to this category. They believe in a personal god who, they believe, will grant them their wishes according to their prayers and material offerings. Some of the wishes seem to get fulfilled while others do not. For unfulfilled wishes they hold destiny responsible. The fulfilled wishes make their faith on the deity stronger and they keep coming back for more. Word spreads and the prayers to that particular deity become more common. Many strivers complain that they have said a lot of prayers but they did not receive the desired fruits. They wonder as to why was God not listening to their prayers.

When one gets tired of praying, he begins to question the God. Such demonstration of prayer and devotion is egoistic and artificial. Expecting prayer and devotion to give you measurable material returns is nothing but greed. The second category of prayer is for devotion and not for any worldly desire. These prayers are only for spiritual objective of liberation. These are meant for personal spiritual growth. Such prayers gradually bring a change to people's mind, their attitude and their view of worldly life, bringing dispassion and detachment. Prayer must emerge from within. Prayer must involve devotion and should only encompass giving and surrender. Surrender does not mean giving up everything that belongs to you. Surrender means giving up the notion of ownership. If prayers don't get answered, one must identify own shortcomings in devotion and try to overcome them. By constantly remaining in attitude of gratitude one remains steadfast on the path of devotion and will soon discover the magical love of God.

God can be realised only by fixation of the mind and intellect in Him. Generally, people think that God can be realised only if they perform virtuous actions, have good conduct, meditate by leading secluded life and so on. Dispassion and detachment are important for all the strivers on the path of devotion. Some strivers believe in physical renouncement and they, therefore, prefer to be in solitude. They believe in moving away from worldly objects. Their physical renouncement may prove to be useful, but by mere renunciation they do not attain perfection. For attaining perfection, dispassion from pleasure and detachment from the body, senses, mind and intellect are essential. When they lead a lonely life away from the world, they are likely to develop an egoistic notion which cannot be removed without getting involved in the welfare of all beings. It is also not possible for striver to always remain in solitude because he has to come in contact with society for the maintenance of his body.

The three paths of seeking union with God, i.e. *Gyanyog, Karmyog and Bhaktiyog*, even though looking different, lead to the same objective. In *karmyog*, one does not consider anyone evil, does not desire evil for anyone and does not do evil to anyone. In *gyanyog*, one accepts the fact that he does not want anything for himself and does not want to do anything for himself. Like a *karmyogi*, it is necessary for a *gyanyogi* to remain engrossed in the welfare of all beings without attachment, to attain perfection. A *karmyogi* regards the bodies i.e. physical, subtle and causal, as belonging to the world, and uses them in rendering service to the world. A gyanyogi identifies himself with Bramh, the Absolute. Thus, a *karmayogi* identifies with the insentient elements while a *gyanyogi* identifies with the sentient. *Karmyog* and *gyanyog* complement each other, in a way. The desire for pleasure can be wiped out by *karmyog* while the desire for knowledge can be satisfied by *gyanyog*.

However, a striver who is firmly established in either of the two gets the fruit of both, i.e. when desire for pleasure is wiped out, the desire for knowledge is satisfied. When the desire for knowledge is satisfied the desire for pleasure is wiped out. In both cases, detachment develops automatically.

In *gyanyog* there is a need to practice *karmyog*, while for karmyog there is no need to practice *gyanyog*, as a pre-requisite. A *karmyogi* is a *sanyasi* or renouncer from the very beginning. The path of *karmyog*, i.e. action, can be followed by everyone and under all circumstances. A *gyanyogi* and a *karmyogi* both have to renounce their affinity for the world. A *gyanyog*i roots out the sense of doership through dispassion and discrimination, while a *karmyogi* discards it by performance of actions for the welfare of others without any desire for fruit of action. If a striver renounces the sense of doership his desire for fruit of action gets renounced; and

if he renounces his desire for fruit of action his sense of doership is renounced. The egoism of a *karmyogi* perishes more quickly and easily because he works for others. The egoism of a *gyanyogi* may continue to exist longer as he holds that he is a seeker of salvation and he works for salvation for himself. It is easy for a *karmyogi* to renounce objects as these will be utilised by others, while it is comparatively more difficult for a *gyanyogi* to renounce them unless his dispassion is very keen.

The supreme state which is attained by the *gyanyogi* is also reached by the *karmyogi*. A *karmyogi*, in order to distinguish sentient from insentient, has to use discrimination of a *gyanyogi*. Similarly, a *gyanyogi* has to adopt method of *karmyog* of not performing action for himself. A *gyanyogi's* discrimination is to be utilised to distinguish the soul from the world and actions of a *karmyogi* are performed in order to render service to the world. Getting detached from one's own body or identifying body with those of others will bear the same fruit.

Karmyogi and *gyanyogi* become free from egoism with the passage of time. But the egoism of a *bhaktiyogi* perishes in the very beginning as he completely surrenders to God. A *bhaktiyogi* possesses the traits of friendliness, compassion etc for all beings which are rarely found in the *karmyogi* and *gyanyogi*. A *bhaktiyogi* regards himself as insignificant from the very beginning. In *karmyog* and *gyanyog* a striver has his own faith or belief and he makes efforts accordingly while a *bhaktiyogi*, depends completely on God, without having any independent faith or belief of his own. He identifies his desire with His desire. He does not worry even to attain salvation or God realisation. He does not worry about his appearance and resources. The Lord provides him with the means for his bodily maintenance.

Comparison, if any, between the three paths is merely from the point of view of ease in practice and possibility of success on that path. *Karmyog* is placed at higher pedestal than *gyanyog* while *bhaktiyog* is placed at higher pedestal than *karmyog*. In *gyanyog*, striver renounces unreal by giving importance to the discrimination between real and unreal. But while renouncing unreal, the entity of the renouncer and the renounced remains for long. That is why complete renouncement of unreal takes a very long time in *gyanyog*. By putting objects into selfless service of others in *karmyog*, it is easier to renounce them. In *bhaktiyog*, by considering the world as belonging to God, it is easiest to renounce the unreal. *Karmyogi* and *gyanyogi* have equanimity but they may not have friendly nature and tenderness while a *bhaktiyogi* has all these qualities from the very beginning. There is predominance of reclusion on the path of *gyanyog* and reclusion is dry.

Therefore, a *gyanyogi* appears to be stern externally because of reclusion and apathy even though he may not be stern from inside. A *bhaktiyogi* is happy and always looks to give happiness to others.

8

DHARMA

II Do perform thy prescribed duty, for action is superior to inaction… Gita 3:8 II

Dharma is to do everything very practically skillfully and for the benefit and well-being of all, without causing any harm to anyone. Dharma means peace and purity of heart. Dharma signifies right behaviour which includes duties, conduct, virtues, and way of living. The activities which are immoral, against nature, unethical, wrong or unlawful, are called adharma. Vātsyāyana has listed dharma and adharma of body, words, and mind. Dharma of body is doing charity, and rendering service to others, including relief to the distressed while adharma of body is violence and theft, of all types. Dharma of words would be in following path of truth, sincerity, and honesty in written as well as spoken words. It also includes speaking with good intention, gentleness, and kindness. Adharma of words is speaking or writing falsehood, caustic talk, making false statements and talking in absurd manner. Dharma of mind is compassion and detachment, while adharma of mind is ill will, covetousness, absence of morals and selfishness. When we value other peoples' needs alongside our own, we are following dharma. When we stay focused on our own needs at the cost of others', we are doing adharma.

The word 'dharma' is often confused with religious belief and religious identification. Dharma implies a sense of moral commitment or obligation to someone or something. There is nothing wrong in following one's faith but by fanatically pursuing one's own chosen path, one forgets the basic duty of action for others. When someone recognises a duty, he commits himself to its fulfilment without considering his own self-interest. Its fulfilment may, however, involve some sacrifice of immediate self-interest.

The bundle of vasanas or impressions with which an individual has arrived into a particular body, is called his *swadharma* or natural duty. The duty of that birth and profession is his swadharma. It is, however, necessary that this duty should not be forbidden in scriptures. If it is not so, it becomes adharma. Now a doubt arises. Should a person born in the family of butcher continue to perform his inherited duty of slaughtering animals? Will he not incur sin? The actions which are harmful and injurious to others cannot be called one's natural duty. A forbidden action is always evil and therefore must be abandoned. A man is born in a family in order to reap fruit of his past actions and exhaust them. He is not born there to commit sins. He is free in making a choice. If his heart becomes pure, he cannot slaughter animals. By calling it a family profession, and therefore his natural duty, and continuing to slaughter animals, he will only accumulate more sins.

The scriptures permit a man to perform two types of actions – ordained actions, i.e. *vihit* karma and stipulated actions, i.e. *niyat* karma. The ordained actions are laid down in scriptures and include fasting, worshipping etc. There are large number of such actions given in the scriptures. However, in everyday life, due to many responsibilities and preoccupations in the material world, it becomes difficult for a person to perform all the ordained actions.

It is, however, relatively easier to abandon forbidden actions, and everyone must endeavour to achieve that. On the other hand, the stipulated actions are those which are performed according to one's circumstances, order of life and nature. These actions are performed to earn a livelihood and to perform all actions related to fulfil one's responsibilities and commitments in life. The duties related to own circumstances and order of life are one's own duty while all other duties are called duties of another. Performance of one's stipulated duty, even though devoid of merit, is always better than the duty of another, well performed. The duty of another may outwardly seem full of merit, be easy to perform, be attractive, provide riches, comforts, honour, praise etc, yet it is forbidden. On the other hand, one's own duty may be difficult to perform, not appealing and not providing riches, comfort, honour, praise etc, yet such duty should be performed without expecting any reward, without ego and without attachment. To remain detached is one's own duty while to be attached is the duty of another. To render selfless service to others is one's own duty while to have desire for fruit is the duty of another. To perform all actions sincerely, honestly and to the best of ability is one's own duty while to be fraudulent, greedy and selfish is the duty of another. To be liberated is one's own duty while to be a pleasure seeker is the duty of another.

The duties of the four varnas which are intrinsic to their nature, are described in the eighteenth chapter of Gita. These duties come naturally to them and they don't face any difficulty in performing them because their temperaments naturally suit these. Serenity, control of senses, austerity, purity, forgiveness, uprightness etc, are duties of *brahmin* intrinsic to his nature. Heroism, radiance, firmness, fearlessness, dexterity, generosity and display of authority, are the natural duties of a *kshatriya*, inherent to his nature.

Agriculture and commerce are the duties of a *vaishya* and actions consisting of service are the duties of a *shudra*, intrinsic to its nature.

9

VARNA CLASSIFICATION

II The fourfold order was created by Me according to the modes of their nature and action....Gita 4:13 II

By evolving ceaselessly, one finally gets to be born as a human on this earth. A being qualifies to be born as a human based on the qualities and actions of his previous birth. Family and the environment given to him in a particular birth is mainly to enable him to receive the fruits of his past karmas and exhaust them. The environment that he gets will be most suitable for his spiritual growth. The temperament that he displays would depend on the impressions gathered by him in the past. He is born with a unique set of skills and behaviour. Family does play an important role but it does not mean that the man will have the talent and the inclinations of the ancestors of his family and that he will naturally perform well in the family profession. There are clear temperamental distinctions recognisable from person to person. These temperamental distinctions have been utilised to classify the humanity into four castes or *varnas*.

In Gita, a brahmin has been called the voice of the Lord's cosmic form. It means that he must impart knowledge and teach and preach the people of the four varnas because he possesses knowledge. A kshatriya has been called arm or hand of the Lord's cosmic form, because he is required to protect people of the four varnas. However, in case of threat to themselves, it becomes the duty of all the four varnas to protect themselves, their kith and kin, as well as their property. A vaishya has been called the stomach of the Lord's cosmic form. As the stomach receives and processes food and nourishes all the limbs, it is the duty of a vaishya to procure commodities, and, according to needs and demands of people, supply these by transporting from one place to another. By agriculture and trade he caters to the needs of all the four varnas. A shudra has been called the foot of the Lord's cosmic form. As feet carry the weight of the entire body, a shudra renders service to the people of all four varnas.

Duties of the four varnas, intrinsic to their nature, are listed in the eighteenth chapter of Gita. A brahmin's duties, intrinsic to his nature are serenity, control of the senses, austerity, purity, forgiveness, uprightness, wisdom and expertise for proper performance of yagya etc. A brahmin who has the predominance of the mode of goodness

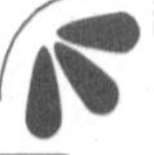

(sattva), naturally possesses these qualities. None of these qualities relate to earning of livelihood. They need others to support them for livelihood or survival. A kshatriya's duties inherent to his nature are bravery, radiance, firmness, dexterity, generosity and authority. Agriculture and commerce are the duties of a vaishya, inherent to his nature and actions consisting of service are the duties of a Shudra, born of his nature.

No one can be said to belong to a caste by birth or by posing as one. These four varnas do not merely represent four types of persons but, more importantly, four types of thoughts and states of mind. The capabilities and the nature of the man were classified into the four varnas so that the swadharm, or natural duty, of the person could be identified which will enable him to make his best contribution to the society. Earlier, in the ashram system of education, all the children were put in the same environment and were carefully observed by their teachers.

After a period of observation, their varna was decided based on their demonstrated capabilities and inclination. It was possible that a kshatriya's child may possess a shrewd business acumen and so the child would be classified into 'vaishya' varna. A vaishya's son may demonstrate brahmin's temperament and therefore would be classified as brahmin. Despite its intrinsic advantages, the system slowly withered away but the system of varna, or caste, became rigid in society.

A hierarchy defining superiority and inferiority of castes was conceived and a social divide was created and exploited. This system that our society suffered for long was flawed because it connected profession with birth. It had political overtones and was utilised as a strong tool to control the society by dividing everyone into four rigid groups. Ignoring individual nature and talent, it was presumed that a brahmin's son will be scholar and a kshatriya's son will automatically be capable of leading and fighting, and so on. Castes were linked to varnas and were assigned to a particular guna. Brahmins were linked to sattva guna, kshatriyas and vaishyas to rajas guna and Shudras were linked to tamas guna. Assigning duties which are not commensurate with the temperament of a verna may, however, create chaos for everyone. A simple brahmin, if asked to run a business, may only incur loss. He may not have shrewdness and cunning necessary to run the show. Gradually, the society has been able to address these misconceptions and the tendency to typecast is diminishing. These old beliefs do not rigidly hold anymore. According to Gita, a man of lower caste possessing virtues of the higher caste, should be regarded as noble even though he is born of a lower womb. A shudra whose conduct is noble, should not be regarded as shudra and a brahmin who does not perform duty of a brahmin, should not be regarded as a Brahmin. It means that it is predominance of action rather than birth which should decide the varna.

People of all varnas are winning gallantry awards and are running businesses well. But even while doing so their basic traits always influence their behaviour.

10

TAMING THE MIND

II Our life is shaped by our mind, for we become what we think : Lord Buddha II

As much as we need exercise for our physical health, we require a regular reflective practice for our mental and emotional well-being. Moments of solitude allow us to slow down the neurotic pace of mental activity. As we learn to observe our recurring thought patterns, we also begin to see the futility of many of our thoughts that usually occupy our mind. Building our reflective capacity strengthens our emotional equilibrium. We are then less easily affected by the daily ups and downs of life. We also become more thoughtful and less reactive in our responses.

Brain and mind have a very complex relationship. Some people believe that the brain and mind are the same and that functions of mind are just another facet of the brain's domain. Actually, brain is a physical organ meant to control the body and its various activities through nervous system while mind is a non-physical entity, responsible for thoughts and awareness. Mind holds the power of imagination, recognition, and appreciation, and is responsible for processing feelings and emotions, resulting in attitudes and actions Brain can be seen while mind is invisible. We can 'change our mind' but we cannot 'change' the brain. Distinction between brain and mind, however, is not so straight forward. Brain and mind do impact each other in many ways.

The most distinct scientific evidence of a strong relationship between the physical brain and the mind is the impact trauma or any physical alterations to the brain have on the mind.

Thought is a faculty of the mind. Mind can create a thought and as per the intensity of the thought, it can influence the brain. This influence can be positive or negative. Mind can lead us to inner hell or inner heaven. It can equally impact the external environment, depending on how we use our mind. We tend to categorise our thoughts as good and bad and this affects our actions and responses. We have power to remain indifferent to these and watch the thoughts like a mere spectator. Thoughts come and go and we should not try to own them. Mind should be constantly occupied in some constructive activity. Situations, by themselves, are never a source of failure; mind is responsible for this. One fails only if mind interprets it as a failure.

While strong mind can bring one back from the jaws of sure defeat, a weak mind can keep us depressed and lead us to doom.

We should carefully select our thoughts, just as we select our clothes every day. Texture of thoughts decides the texture of our mind. We never dress shabbily, so why should we wear shabby thoughts. Love, compassion, mercy, trust etc give positive vibes while ego, anger, criticism, jealousy, hatred, revenge, rejection, depression give negative vibes. The vibes create matching thoughts which draw the mind in their direction. Thoughts created by us affect not only us but also the people around us or those connected with us. We should, therefore, be constantly alert to thought-hygiene and keep checking thoughts to keep them positive all the time.

A sound mind in a sound body, goes the proverb. This has led many to believe that sound body will naturally possess a sound mind. The connection is not so direct

and it is not necessary that a sound mind will lead to a sound body or vice-versa. A healthy body needs nutritious food and exercise. Similarly for mind to be healthy a diet of positive thoughts and exercise in the form of meditation is needed. Even a healthy body will only enforce demoniac actions if the mind is under the influence of any negativity. A sound mind, on the other hand, can display its brilliance even in a frail body. Posture of mind is more important than physical posture.

Emotion is often associated with mood, temperament, personality, disposition and motivation. All emotions are generated in the mind as per external stimulus. Negative emotions, if not handled properly, have the potential to increase our stress level. They can hamper our enthusiasm for life depending on how long we let them affect us and the way we choose to express them. On the other hand, excessive positive emotions can affect our judgement and make us miss out

on crucial facts. For emotional stability, we should never react suddenly to everything that the external environment presents to us. It would be wise to first think, try to find the facts, assess the situation and then give opinion or take action. We should endeavour to pick positivity even in negative and adverse situations. Mahatma Gandhi used to receive many letters which were full of negativity and foul words for him. He would simply throw such letters into waste bin but before doing that he would remove the pin which he could use later.

Mind is perceived as a continuous flow of thoughts. These thoughts pertain to our past experience or future dreams. Anger, greed, stress etc, resulting from our desires, create turbulence and agitation in our mind, leading to loss of mental peace. When we attach ourselves to a specific thought, we stay attached to it and join the flow to whichever direction it takes us. We should remain alert and observant of our thoughts. We should create a mental vastness, like an ocean, so that worldly desires are not able to create emotional agitations and we achieve a state of inner silence and peace. It is necessary to introspect and watch the mind carefully. We should not allow the mind to dissipate energy uselessly on vain thoughts, worries, imaginations and fears.

It is worth examining as to why the mind wanders. Once a worldly desire is born, man begins to consider all the possible ways to fulfil it. These methods become the branches of the same desire. Senses tempt the mind towards sense objects while intellect guides it to be aware of the consequences. A sort of struggle goes on in the mind. Disturbance resulting from this struggle, becomes an obstacle to concentration.

Mind is like a child. As a child needs to be monitored all the time, same should be done with the mind too. The child will go on crying and howling and finally may break something in anger or put himself into danger. Mind may similarly create negative thoughts. Being inquisitive and playful all the time, a child can put himself into a dangerous situation. Mind can also be mischievous and take the brain in the wrong direction. This will start a chain of wrong thoughts and lead to harmful consequences. Man will not even realise that he is on the wrong path. We can control our emotional outcomes caused by external triggers, provided we have control over our mind. Lord Krishna says that one who has acquired the skills to manage his mind is capable of executing any worldly activity in a most efficient manner. Lord further explains that one can achieve control of the mind through continuous practice and with a sense of vairagya, detachment.

Turning inward is the only way If we truly want to achieve success in our journey from soul to the Supersoul, Yogik system speaks of attending to our self-created walls of resistance. When we start offloading the wasteful desires, our mind will become

silent, still and pure and the wall of ego will begin to disintegrate. Controlling the urge for sense-objects is important but it is not necessary to deny all sense-objects. It is wrong to resort to self-denial and self-punishment. Controlling the mind will automatically lead to dispassion towards sense-objects and continuous practice will make successful meditation possible.

We routinely judge ourselves in comparison to others. We continuously experience a sense of lack because we are always thinking about what we don't have rather than be grateful for all that we do have. It heightens our inner insecurity if the other person is richer, stronger and more successful. Ego gets fanned if the other person is weaker. For a quieter mind we need to get comfortable living by our personal values and inner yardsticks of evaluation rather than any external comparisons. Have faith that whatever happens, is for the highest good. Trust that whatever you have got is what you deserved to get.

Mindfulness is a technique to keep the mind in the present and it is a very effective method of mastering the mind. Mindfulness needs to be practiced and should become a way of life. Once we achieve that, we will constantly be in the blissful state and mind's drift will be controlled. My boss at Pune would allow his officers to come and sit in his office while he was busy in a file or other paperwork but would attend to us only once he had mindfully finished the work he had in hand at that point in time. Thereafter he would give us undivided attention.

Regulating the breathing will calm the mind and improve concentration. The breath that we inhale is called '*apaan vayu*' and the breath we exhale is called '*prana vayu*'. Normally the speed of *prana vayu* is faster than the speed of *apaan vayu*. In order to regulate the process of inhalation and exhalation so that these may take equal time, first the *apaan vayu* is inhaled through the left nostril and then the *prana vayu* is exhaled through the right nostril. Then the *apaan vayu* is inhaled through the right nostril and the *prana vayu* is exhaled through the left nostril. This process is popularly known as *anulom-vilom*. Through constant practice the flow of *prana* and *apaan vayu* becomes even, gentle, subtle or thin. When there is no sensation of air inside or outside the nostril and in the throat etc, it should be understood that flow of *prana* and *apaan vayu* has become even.

Meditation helps in improving concentration and achieving mindfulness. It requires us to notice and understand all kinds of thoughts, feelings and actions without judgment or criticism. Complete your important tasks or remove their thought from the mind and then start the meditation with a calm mind. Find a comfortable seat where you can sit up tall either cross legged on the floor or in a chair.

Keep neck, head and the back in a straight position so that the spinal cord may remain erect. Close your eyes or soften your gaze so that you are not focussing on anything in particular. Place your hands, palm down, on the top of your thighs. Exhale air forcibly from lungs two or three times and then hold the breath as long as one can. Now start breathing slowly and come to a natural state of breathing. By doing so, the pursuits and distractions of the mind disappear. Gently close eyes and bring attention to the sensations of breathing near the nostrils or to the movement of the abdomen when breathing in and out. Don't try to control breathing, but simply be aware of your natural breathing rhythm. Notice the sensation of sitting, become aware of the ground or the chair beneath you, and the parts of the body in contact with it. Bring your focus onto the hands, noticing their weight on your thighs, and the sensation of the fabric of your cloth.

Notice how your breath feels in your body as you inhale and exhale. Make no effort to change your breath, simply let your breath flow in and out.

The link between energy, breath and mind is such that if you agitate one, the other two become agitated and if you calm one, the other two also calm down. Breath is the easiest of these three linked elements to control. Control your breath and see how quickly it influences your thoughts. Aim to stay focussed on these sensations of the breath when the mind wanders, acknowledge them and come back to the breath. Even if a thought comes to mind, don't fight it and don't push it away forcibly. All projections and distractions of the mind are transient, so if they are born, they would certainly decay. Clouds appear and disappear in the sky but the sky remains the same. If some thought crops up, we should remain neutral and indifferent. The thought, being transitory in nature, will disappear on its own. Stored thoughts begin to come out at the time of meditation, because when one was busy with other things these could not find an outlet. Their pace of appearance will gradually reduce and finally stability and focus will be achieved. With the disappearance of attachment and aversion we can attain peace which is spontaneous. Slowly and with practice we will achieve mindfulness in everything that we do and we will feel happy and stable under all circumstances.

There is notion that meditation can be practised only in isolated places like jungles and in the caves etc. A person engaged in day-to-day activities can practice meditation equally well. Having physically isolated himself for solitude deep into a forest, man is actually in a crowd if he is unable to leave behind his preoccupation with the worldly things and sense-objects. True meditation is, being in the present, not getting carried away by the thoughts of the past and worries of the future, being aware of your surroundings and

alert to your circumstances and not getting attached to any of them. Finally, it should not be mandatory anymore to sit down to meditate but be in that state all the time. We will find our efficiency increasing manifold and effortlessly.

11

FOOD AND FASTING

II Fasting is not just a physical discipline: it can be a spiritual feast II

Food is any substance consumed to provide nutritional support to the body. Food provides essential nutrients, such as carbohydrates, fats, proteins, vitamins, and minerals. The substance is ingested and assimilated by the cells to provide energy, maintain life and stimulate growth. Food that we partake is also linked with our guna.

What we choose to eat gives out what we are, how we think and behave. The foods which promote life, vitality, strength, health, joy and cheerfulness and the foods which are juicy, bland, nourishing and agreeable, are dear to sattvik people. These foods provide strength and nourishment to the body and give purity and happiness. The foods which are bitter, sour, salty, very hot, pungent, dry, and scorching, are liked by rajas people. Such foods produce pain, grief and disease. When the texture of thought improves, the individual finds himself changing his tastes. His choice of food is totally revolutionised to give him full satisfaction. Food which is half cooked or half ripe, insipid, stale, polluted and impure, is dear to the tamas people.

The feelings of a person who receives and of the person who offers food, also have their effect on food. Food which is offered and received with great pleasure and respect is of superior value and is very satisfying. The food offered with pleasure but not

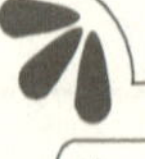

received happily by the person consuming, and without gratitude, is considered of medium value. Food offered with a feeling of compulsion and as a forced burden, and received similarly by the person consuming it, becomes of inferior value.

Sattvik people earn their livelihood by honest means, and they cook their food by wearing clean clothes in a well cleaned and pure kitchen. Their food is first offered to God and then eaten with a feeling of gratitude to the Almighty. Rajasik people, while earning livelihood, do not care if it is by using fair means or foul. They maintain cooking hygiene but they consume food for taste and fashion. The persons having dominant tamasik guna do not hesitate to earn food by foul means such as falsehood, fraud, theft and robbery etc. They cook without any sense of purity and cleanliness, and without paying attention to the manner in which food is cooked.

It is necessary to discuss fasting while talking of intake. Normally, fasting is understood as giving up food for duration of a few hours, a day or more. But the term fasting does not imply rationalising digestive system alone. It is much more than not eating. Fasting is an important tool for physical, mental, emotional and spiritual health. There are four different tools for deriving maximum benefit from fasting.

The first, of course, is fasting of food. Human body is not an eating machine. Uncontrolled eating will only make one sick. We should eat only when our digestive fire actually burns and asks for it, not when our tongue yearns for it. Eat right to enhance immunity.

The second fasting is fasting of breath. Quick breathing due to physical exercise may be good for the body but quick breathing as a result of anger, stress and other negative emotions is harmful.

More heat an engine produces, the faster it burns out. Every cell is like an engine that is being powered by intake of breath. Slow inhalations and long exhalations, with breath pauses, will keep one stress free. With breath fasting, one ages slowly and the thoughts become more positive.

The third fasting is of speech where we fast on hurtful and pessimistic speech. This fasting is not occasional but should be practiced all the time. We should consciously speak words that are true and cause joy to others in a very pleasing tone. This fasting is very good for improving and sustaining relations.

The fourth fasting is the fasting of movement. It is not about lying down on your cushion but fasting on the wasteful agility of the mind. It means sitting still, either observing your breath, listening to the sound of nature. Sit still. Spend time with yourself and introspect.

Even if we can sit still for one minute at a time, it will bring down the restlessness in our body and mind and will help us in becoming a better person.

12

YAGYA

II Life itself is yagya II

Yagya literally means worship, devotion, prayer, a form of offering or oblation, and sacrifice. Yagya is not merely lighting of holy fire, chanting of mantras and making symbolic sacrifice into the fire to please the gods who have been invoked though the specified mantras. Every aspect of life can be yagya. Every activity should be performed as yagya and as a duty, without any desire for a particular fruit.

Actions performed according to one's order of life and circumstances, in accordance with the ordinance of scriptures and without expecting any fruits are yagya. Everyone can perform yagya in his or her sphere of activity. Rearing the children well, providing for their needs, setting good examples and imparting good values in them is the yagya for the parents. Prescription of medicine for patients with the sole aim of restoring patient's health and reducing his suffering, is yagya for a physician. Studying sincerely and gaining all round knowledge is yagya for students. Honest business done for the welfare of others can be regarded as yagya performed by a businessman. Sacrifice, oblation, charity, and penance are important elements of all types of yagya. These can, however, take different forms for different activities.

When we are born into this world, everything necessary for our life is already made available. Parents bring us into this

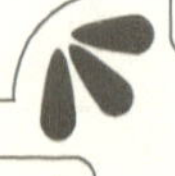

world, foster and guide us. Preceptors and teachers help us in our quest for knowledge. There are many others who play an important role in shaping us. No action is possible in this world without help from others. Whatever power, success, rank, authority, material, wealth and property etc that we possess, we owe it all to others. So, it would be proper to devote these to their service. Actions so performed selflessly for the welfare of others are also yagya.

For some people Bramh is the resource, cause for all action, action itself and also the outcome of all action. For them, all yagyas arise from Bramh in which Bramh is the performer offering Bramh, the material, to the sacred fire which is also nothing other than Bramh, invoking but Bramh. While partaking food they remember that it is Bramh eating Bramh, they are offering to Bramh the food that is Bramh, invoking nothing but grace of Bramh. All actions performed with this type of thought are the finest yagya, leading to realisation.

Restraining the senses is also yagya. The yagya of senses means that even when the objects of senses come in contact with the senses, the senses remain free from attraction and repulsion. To control senses, a striver may choose to live in solitude, chant mantras and meditate. Or, he may move about among the sense objects with the mind, intellect, ego and the senses free from attraction and repulsion. Both methods are useful but solitude may not be very effective because striver is prone to attraction and repulsion when he returns among the worldly objects for the maintenance of his body and his survival. When the striver becomes free of attraction and repulsion, he remains the same in solitude as well as in practical life. Such strivers sacrifice all the functions of senses into the fire of yagya of self-restraint.

Yagya of life-breath implies control over inhaling and exhaling process through sacrifice of life breath into life breath. With breath control we come to gain a perfect mastery over the activities of prana in us. Prana is normally misunderstood to mean merely the air we breathe. Besides energising the physiological functions of the body, prana also controls the capacity of a living creature to improve himself in his mental outlook and intellectual life. Water, food and air nurture the body but it is the prana which provides the necessary energy to run it. Prana is life and the air is essential to sustain it. The air enters our organism through the process of inhalation. Then by special channels of subtle energy it spreads itself through the whole organism as life air. It enters the active psychic centers, called chakras. In some chakras this life air may function more actively and in the other ones it may be weaker. Weak functioning of prana in certain area of the body points to the presence of an ailment in the area. Awakening a chakra means re-energising it. The consciousness controls the movement of life air in the organism. Balance in the life air inside the organisms results in healthy body and it becomes easier to control the mind. This yagya helps in channelising the prana energy and brings the activities of life under the perfect control of the individual.

Sacrifice or *ahuti*, given in any form of yagya, is sattvik, if it is offered according to spiritual law by those who expect no reward and believe firmly that to do so is their duty. Parental duty performed as a personal duty as well as social responsibility and without the expectation of return from the children, is sattvik. If the sacrifice is offered in expectation of reward or for the sake of show-off, it is rajasik. Sacrifice which is not in conformity with the ordinances of scriptures and is without faith, is tamasik. While performing our duty as a yagya, we should ensure that the established tenets of dharma are sustained and protected. In the story of Mahabharat, Bhishm took a difficult vow of not marrying and of dedicating himself to the protection of the throne of Hastinapur and its occupant. He made the *ahuti* or sacrifice of his entire life to fulfil his vow, commendably. He performed all his duties as yagya. He did not expect anything in return. He led a devout life and ensured best of the training for all the princes, without bias and showered his affection, equally. But while doing so, he ignored the wrongdoings and injustice perpetrated by the king. He had a very exalted position in the king's court but never put his foot down to prevent adharma which would have prevented the great war, in which millions were killed in just eighteen days. Not doing anything wrong himself is one thing but not preventing wrong things from being done, despite having power to do so, is disillusion and cannot be called a yagya.

13

SANYAS, PENANCE AND DONATION

II Renunciation, and renunciation alone, is the real secret of all realisation....... Swami Vivekanand II

Sanyas or renunciation, does not mean adopting a life of deprivation and misery. Sanyas is a mental attitude, not a physical state. People walk away from home and possessions in the name of renouncement. Renouncement does not mean giving up possessions. One has to renounce dependence, attachment and acquisitiveness and not possessions. Renunciation of attachment for the fruit of action is the seed of Karmyoga. A striver should be attached neither to virtuous or extraordinary actions nor should he have an aversion for evil and ordinary actions. Actions will be over but attachment and aversion will remain and these will lead to bondage. A striver should resolve to relinquish forbidden actions rather than perform prescribed actions, otherwise he will feel proud of performing prescribed actions and his egoism will remain.

There are four views on what all must be given up to attain renunciation. The first view states that we must give up actions which are prompted by desire because desire leads to attachment and then to its fruit. But, even if actions are not performed, the desire may remain. Because of this, doership will remain and hence renouncement cannot be complete. The second view states that abandonment of fruit of action is real renunciation. It is, however, not possible for anyone to abandon fruit of action because it is not in anyone's control. If desire remains, fruit will follow, inevitably. So, it is the desire which must be relinquished, and the desire-prompted actions and resultant fruits will get renounced automatically. The third view recommends that for renunciation, all action must be given up. It is, however, not possible to give up all action. Action is necessary even to sustain our body. The fourth view recommends that acts of charity and penance are not to be given up. This view, however, does not state what other actions should be given up. The list will be very long. So, all the four views appear to be imperfect. In fact, for renunciation, we only need to perform actions relinquishing attachment and desire for fruit.

In the context of *sanyas*, it is normally interpreted that abandonment and renunciation are synonymous. Abandonment is giving up, withdrawing from or relinquishing the anxiety related to fruits-of-action. Abandonment is the step leading to renunciation. Renunciation is total giving up of the desire induced actions. Abandonment is *tyaag* while renunciation is *sanyas*. Abandonment, however, does not mean giving up one's duty. Everyone has his own obligations to himself and to others in the society. It is a sin to abandon the assigned as well as obligatory duty.

Out of ignorance or lack of proper thinking, an individual may ignore his obligations and refuse to serve the world he is living in. If one's duty is abandoned out of delusion, it is tamasik abandonment and if it is abandoned in order to gain pleasure and rest, it is rajasik abandonment. But if the duty is discharged by abandoning the desire for fruit and also attachment for it, it is sattvik abandonment. A sattvik abandonment is the real abandonment on the path of renunciation. If giving up worldly possessions amounted to renunciation, every

person would attain salvation at the time of death because at that moment one abandons all the worldly possessions including the body. The internal abandonment of attachment and desire etc is the real abandonment which frees a man from bondage.

Persons with dominant rajasik guna consider penance and charity painful because there are many restrictions in performing these. They have to spend lot of money and have to suffer hardships by foregoing bodily comfort. They want to lead a carefree life by abandoning activities which involve physical and mental effort. Even if the rajasik person demonstrates some interest in performance of charity etc he does it to show off. Such a person can never reach renunciation. In sattvik relinquishment actions are not abandoned but are performed carefully and promptly, without expecting any reward. Disagreeable actions may be abandoned but there should be no aversion towards them. Aversion amounts to attachment leading to bondage. The man who has no aversion to disagreeable action, and no attachment to an agreeable one, is a man of true renunciation. It may not be possible for all of us to achieve sattvik type of relinquishment but we should endeavour to shed our concerns for the fruit of our actions.

Another method that some strivers use for renunciation is penance or *tapasya*. For this they go into isolation away from reach of general public. They start living a frugal life and life of deprivation. Some of them start tormenting their bodies for austerity. They remain hungry for a long time, lie on thorns or nails with bare bodies, stand on one leg and perform many other violent austerities. This violent form of devotion is very harmful. Their entire attention is focussed on their bodies only and they remain attached to it. They do not perform any other activity. They do not serve the world in which they are living. Gita does not recommend such practices at all. Gita defines austerity performed with foolish stubbornness or self-torture or harming others as demoniac and full of ignorance. Austerity is not about inflicting self-punishment – it is about self-control of the senses.

Using austerity and deprivation as tools for penance or tapasya is a waste of effort. Instead of torturing self in the name of penance one should carry out penance of body, speech and mind and should seek inner peace. Gita has held penance of body as worship of gods and respect of brahmins, elders, teachers with purity and uprightness. Their worship consists in carrying out their orders, following their principles and treating them with reverence from the heart. Practice of celibacy and ahimsa are also important for penance of body. Keeping the words soft, truthful, and pleasant which convey a clear thought process, is the penance of speech. The words which are altogether free from violence, envy, jealousy, and enmity etc and which are full of love, compassion,

forgiveness, generosity and which do not harm anyone, are very beneficial to the person speaking as well as to the person listening. Penance of mind requires keeping it cheerful, gentle, calm and under self-control. Cheerfulness obtained through material objects is temporary but the inner happiness remains permanent and keeps the mind serene and calm. Inner calm can be achieved through inner silence. Circumstances which we term as favourable and unfavourable, will also occur at intervals. The key to inner calm is to achieve equanimity under all circumstances.

The penance of body, speech and mind performed by a person of balanced mind without the expectation of any reward is called sattvik penance. The complete three-fold penance is possible only in sattvik penance. Penance performed in order to gain respect, honour, and reverence and for the sake of show is said to be rajasik penance. Rajasik penance does get the striver respect,

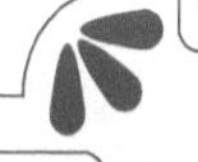

honour, and praise among the people around him but it will not get him any divine results. He cannot be placid and cheerful because his mind is constantly occupied with his own personal achievements and recognition. Tamasik penance is performed with obstinacy, self-torture or by causing injury to others.

Charity or donation is part of renunciation and penance. By leaving all possessions behind and going away to jungles and isolated places, one fails to make any contribution to the society. We should live within the society and develop the habit of charity. Donation may take various forms including donation of money, alms, services, or goods such as clothing, food, medicine, vehicles, blood, organ, emotions and knowledge etc. It is, however, important to know what donation to give, when to give, how much to give, whom to give. Ideally, it should be given to those who have neither done good to the donor nor is there any possibility of getting any return in future. Otherwise, it cannot be considered as donation or charity.

Rajasik people donate at places of pilgrimage, on sacred occasions etc, but their donation or charity is always for reward or to earn a goodwill to be encashed later. Rajasik person first thinks of the man to whom he is indebted or from whom he expects a reward, and then he donates. At times rajasik people donate under compulsion or force. They give because others are doing so or to sustain an image or to satisfy their ego. A charity or donation which is given at a wrong place and time, to an unworthy person, without respect or given with contempt, is called tamasik. Out of delusion the tamasik people do not attach any importance to proper place and time.

A donation of food, water, clothes, and medicine should be made to a needy recipient without much thinking about whether the recipient is worthy or unworthy and whether the place and time are auspicious

or not. Similarly, the act of freeing a man from fear and torture is a gift of fearlessness which should always be made. Quantum of donation is to be restricted to the need of the recipient. We should be careful that an unworthy person is given only so much of food and water that would meet his immediate requirement. He is likely to misuse it if he is given more.

Giving should not be restricted to family and friends only. In such a giving, reciprocation is expected and if that reciprocation does not happen or if it falls short of expectation, it invariably leads to acrimony. There are other forms of donation and charity also. If encouraging someone improves their blood flow, it amounts to blood donation. Carrying out physical activity to help someone in crisis can be called donation of labour or *shram-daan*. Having a habit of not wasting food or water amounts to *ann-daan* and *jal-daan*. Charity or selfless social work at the time of crisis like natural disaster, spread of a disease etc should be done without hesitation and to the best of one's ability. On such occasions, there is no fixed time or quantity as to when and how much we should donate.

14

SOME QUERIES

There are always some queries in the mind of a striver, answers for which may not be available in one location, anywhere. An attempt has been made to answer a few of them. The clarifications are only indicative. To get more detailed explanations, one will have to dive deeper into ocean of Gita and pick pearls for themselves.

Q: Desire for material objects is harmful. But how can we render service without desiring for objects?

A: He who attaches importance to objects, cannot render service with those because he will have pride in doing so and, thus, unknowingly derive pleasure out of his action. Service with material objects is a gross type of service. Real service is rendered through feeling rather than actions. We can render service even with limited resources that we may have.

Q: It is said in scriptures that whenever there has been excess of sins on the earth, Lord appears in his incarnation and destroys the demons who get salvation immediately. So, if we go on committing sins, Lord will himself have to come to kill us. If it is so, we shall also attain salvation easily.

A: It is an interesting argument but we must remember that as per scriptures, Lord destroys only those wicked who cannot be destroyed by anyone else. If we are killed by someone, or die a natural death while performing sinful actions, how would our desire of being killed by Lord be fulfilled?

Due to your desire, you would certainly end up accumulating sins and appropriate fruit for yourself.

Q: Since Lord knows the future of all beings, it can be construed that the man's bondage and emancipation are all predestined. Then why should a man make efforts to attain salvation or emancipation?

A: Man takes birth with the set of past impressions and the bundle of all the karmas, for which he has to receive fruit in this birth. These fruits will appear in the form of circumstances. In every situation, man has the choice of action. It is the freedom given by God. With effort, man can even change his destiny. Emancipation or bondage will depend on the path chosen by the man himself. The only thing predetermined is the fruit which the man will have to bear in the current birth, and he will have no control on it. Man is free to utilise the circumstances to his advantage on his spiritual journey. Effort and action are left to the man.

Q: How can the soul, which is sentient, become the onlooker of the insentient intellect, because an onlooker can only see objects of its own class?

A: The soul identifies itself with the insentient matter and accepts its own separate entity as 'I am'. This 'I' is neither sentient nor insentient. By identifying itself with matter it says, 'I am rich or I am learned'. By identifying with the consciousness, it says, 'I am Bramh'. Thus, the embodied soul has both the portions, the sentient and the insentient. The sentient portion attracts him towards the Lord and the insentient portion, because of its identity with matter attracts him towards the matter and thus he becomes the onlooker of intellect, mind and senses. This assumed identity or affinity is the root of all evils.

Q: What is the difference between sudden death and untimely death?

A: If a man dies of snake bite or by falling (not jumping) from a roof or by drowning, heart failure or by an accident etc, this is sudden death which is predestined. Such a man dies after completing the duration of his life. If a man commits suicide by hanging himself or by jumping into a well or fire or by poisoning himself etc, this is untimely death. A man commits suicide without completing his span of life. He, who commits suicide, incurs the sin of murder and this is a new sin. Sometimes a person, who makes an attempt to commit suicide, survives. Birth of a would-be-child, a good which is likely to be done by him to the people, award of fruit of past actions that is going to be reaped by him because of his past actions, may, however, save him from dying.

Q: Is it true that mind can be controlled only if we don't try to control it?

A: People make lot of efforts in trying to control the mind but are not successful.

Actually, we should neither try to stop the mind from going in a particular direction nor try to force it in another direction. Mind should be left to its own machinations. The thoughts will flow continuously. Our attempts to control it do not influence the mind and its agility, in any way. We make the mistake of attaching ourselves to the thoughts and then hope to control the mind. By trying to eliminate thoughts, we only end up making them stronger. Mind is powerful enough to make you join the flow and then make you jump from thought to thought, at its own pace. We must learn to ignore the mind and learn to remain neutral. All type of thoughts will get eliminated slowly. We can control the mind by not trying to control it. Same is true for controlling senses. In this context, instead of trying to control them, we should make sure that we do not get controlled by them. We should endeavour to stay neutral and detached.

Q: If getting a desired object gives us happiness, why is it said that desire is the root cause of unhappiness?

A: Once we desire any worldly object, we feel happy when we get it. The happiness, actually, does not come from getting the desired object but from the fact that our desire has been fulfilled. Objects, by themselves, cannot make anyone happy or unhappy. For example, when we desire money, we develop attachment to it. The desire becomes strong and the mind gets caught up with money. An obsession begins to develop. Now, when we get the desired money, the money grabbed by the mind gets released and we feel happy. Man commits the mistake of believing that happiness has come because the money has been received. He, now, starts desiring for more and thus bind himself further.

Q: If we state that the Lord is in us, will that make the Lord and us, two different entities?

A: It is our egoistic notion which makes us seem different from God. When Ganges is flooded, water overflows its banks. It also fills the pits which are near the banks. This stagnant water soon becomes dirty. Several germs and insects are born in it. When this water again mixes with the mainstream of Ganges, its impurity and stagnation go away and it again becomes pure and holy water of the Ganges. Similarly, when a man out of his egoistic notion loses inclination for God, he is full of several impurities, such as hatred, enmity, disquietude, unevenness, limitedness, inertness and unholiness etc. But when again he takes refuge in God, all his impurities perish. The reason is that being a fragment of God, he is free from defects. It is because of his egoistic notion that defects had developed in him.

Q: To attain emancipation, is it essential to remove our flaws?

A: Man strongly believes that removing flaws is essential for emancipation. But it is not possible to attain God by employing worldly ways of getting material objects. Yes, removal of flaws will certainly improve our approach and outlook in life. All the flaws are in the perishable body while it is Self which needs emancipation to merge with the God element. Self is unblemished and the flaws are assumed. As we progress on our spiritual journey, we find that the assumed blemishes are reducing gradually. While the flaws reduce, there is no effect on the Self. This establishes that the flaws or defects have no connection with Self. Similarly, we should identify unblemished Self in others also and treat them accordingly.

Q: Why do good and saintly people suffer while the evil persons have a good time?

A: The circumstances that appear in our lives are the fruit of our past karma. Man is at complete liberty to utilise these to reduce his baggage of accumulated karma. The apparent good time that the evil persons appear to enjoy is a fruit of their past karma.

They fail to utilise the favourable situations for converting their karma into akarma. The evil actions being performed in current birth are fresh actions for which they would get fruit later on. The saintly people do not perform any evil actions in the current birth. Moreover, the apparent suffering that they undergo is further reducing their accumulated karma. The suffering is actually not a suffering for the saintly persons because they take everything as God's blessing.

www.ingramcontent.com/pod-product-compliance
Lightning Source LLC
La Vergne TN
LVHW041217150826
845673LV00001B/437

* 9 7 9 8 8 9 1 3 3 4 0 1 4 *